CAMPAIGN 74

THE RHINELAND
1945

THE LAST KILLING GROUND IN THE WEST

SERIES EDITOR: LEE JOHNSON

CAMPAIGN 74

THE RHINELAND 1945

THE LAST KILLING GROUND IN THE WEST

TEXT BY
KEN FORD

BATTLESCENE PLATES BY
TONY BRYAN

Editor: Anita Hitchings
Design: The Black Spot

Colour birds-eye view illustrations by the Black Spot
Cartography by the Map Studio
Battlescene artwork by Tony Bryan
Wargaming the Rhineland by Angus Konstam
Originated by Grasmere Digital Imaging Ltd, Leeds, UK
Printed in China through World Print Ltd.

00 01 02 03 04   10 9 8 7 6 5 4 3 2 1

For a catalogue of all books published by Osprey Military, Automotive and
Aviation please contact:

The Marketing Manager, Osprey Direct UK, PO Box 140,
Wellingborough, Northants, NN8 4ZA, United Kingdom.
Tel. (0)1933 443863, Fax (0)1933 443849.
Email: info@ospreydirect.co.uk

The Marketing Manager, Osprey Direct USA, PO Box 130,
Sterling Heights, MI 48311-0130, USA.
Tel. 810 795 2763, Fax 810 795 4266.
Email: info@ospreydirectusa.com

Visit Osprey at:
www.ospreypublishing.com

KEY TO MILITARY SYMBOLS

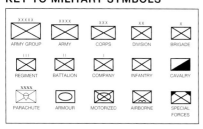

Artist's Note

PAGE 2: **Three British commanders of 'Veritable' discuss the
forthcoming attack on Goch: FM Bernard Montgomery
(British 21st Army Group), LtGen Brian Horrocks (British
XXX Corps) and MajGen G. Ivor Thomas (43rd 'Wessex'
Division). Horrocks had served with Monty in North Africa
before he was seriously wounded at Bizerta. Thomas'
Wessex Division was continuously in the thick of the
fighting after landing in Normandy, and by the end of the
war had suffered more casualties than any other British
infantry division. (Imperial War Museum)**

PAGE 3: **Mounted troops from the 1st SS Panzer Division
'Leibstandarte Adolf Hitler' pass an American M3 half-track
which had been commandeered by other men of the division
during the Ardennes offensive. The division had fought in
most of the German theatres of the war, from Poland and
France in 1940, through the Russian and Italian campaigns
to Normandy in 1944. Twice completely rebuilt after
suffering dreadful casualties, the Liebstandarte Division was
seen as Hitler's 'fire brigade', often called in to the worst
areas of the fighting to stabilise forces under pressure.
During the Ardennes attack, the division formed part of
'Sepp' Dietrich's 6th Panzer Army. (Imperial War Museum)**

CONTENTS

THE RHINELAND: GERMAN AND ALLIED POSITIONS AT START OF OFFENSIVE

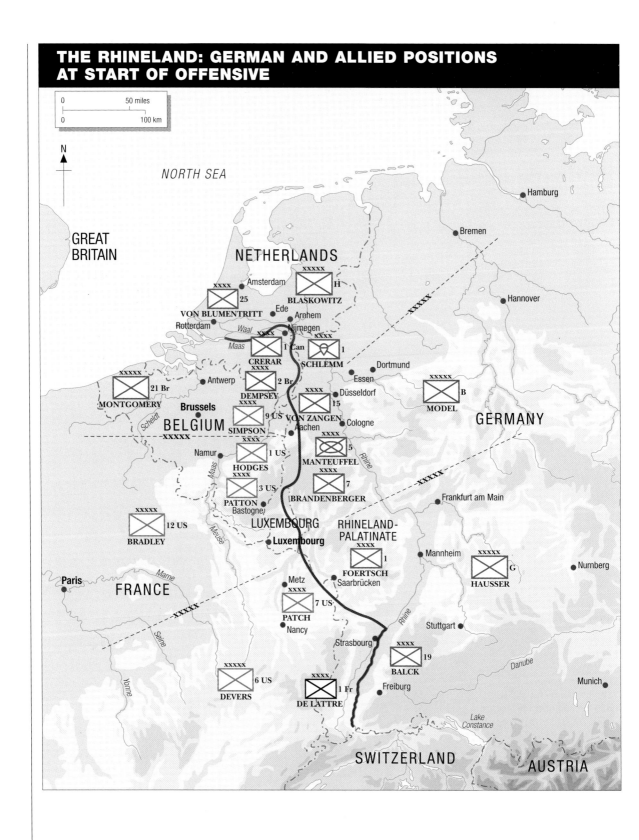

ORIGINS OF THE BATTLE

On 16 January 1945, the German forces which had undertaken Hitler's last big offensive in western Europe found themselves back at their start line. The massive Ardennes assault was to have pushed the Allies beyond the Meuse and split the British and American forces in half; but it had failed miserably, with losses of over 100,000 men. Hitler's gamble to seize the initiative had failed; all German energy and effort would now have to be geared to the defence of the homeland.

The Allied armies under the supreme command of Gen Dwight D. Eisenhower had, by the start of 1945, arrived at the German border and they stretched from The Netherlands to the Swiss frontier. Below Strasbourg Gen Devers' US 6th Army Group had actually pushed the Germans back to the River Rhine. Elsewhere, the front line either confronted the German Siegfried defensive line (Hitler's Westwall) or rested on other river barriers. North of Aachen, Gen Simpson's US 9th Army had breached the Siegfried Line, but was stalled in front of the River Roer, while Gen Dempsey's British 2nd Army was lined up along the River Maas. In the far north, in Holland, Gen Crerar's Canadian 1st Army held a bridgehead between the Maas and the Rhine overlooking German soil – a legacy of the failed Arnhem campaign – but was confronted with one of the strongest sectors of the Siegfried Line.

To the German people the River Rhine is the mythical border of Germany. It is the river of legend, of Lorelei, of brave Roland and

During the Ardennes operation, this Tiger Mk II from the 501st SS Heavy Tank Battalion was abandoned on the Stavelot road due to a lack of fuel. American engineers inspect the perfectly sound tank. At this time in the war Germany was suffering great shortages of fuel and Hitler's December offensive was designed to overrun American supply dumps and capture new stocks. The plan was not a great success and the lack of fuel was always a great problem for the units involved in the operation.
(Imperial War Museum)

Siegfried. The Rhine is an important symbol of German history and national strength. During Roman times it formed the barrier between the civilised world and the barbarians. In later times, when Germans ruled both sides of the river, it was an important psychological barrier and a vital military objective. As long as the river protected the country from invasion from the west, the German people could keep alive the hope that all was well. In front of the Rhine, between the river and the borders of France, Belgium, Luxembourg and The Netherlands, was the Rhineland. This strip of land had had a chequered past, having been hotly contested throughout history. It had been much disputed during the Thirty Years War, and again in Napoleonic times when the Emperor had pushed the borders of Germany back to the old Roman frontier. Germany retook the territory after the Franco-Prussian War only to have it seized again by France after World War I. In 1940, Germany brought the area back under its domination. In February 1945, the invading Allied armies were poised to take possession of the Rhineland away from the Germans.

The object of the Rhineland campaign of 1945 was to push all German forces back across the Rhine or destroy them in front of the river. Once the river line had been brought under control, preparations could be made for an assault crossing. Eisenhower had decided on a 'broad front' policy in which all of his troops would advance along the whole of his line, rather than focus all of his forces in one particular sector. No crossings would be made of the Rhine until the whole of the Allied Army was in possession of the west bank of the river. It was a policy that was not universally approved, and one which has been called into question by historians ever since. It was, none the less, a strategy that was ultimately successful.

The 'broad front' policy evolved with the progress of the war after the Normandy landings. Initially, pre-invasion planners had envisioned two major thrusts into Germany, each heading for great industrial areas in order to smash the bulk of the German manufacturing capability. One was to pass north of the Ardennes aiming at the Ruhr, while the other was to go south of the Ardennes to eliminate the lesser Saar industrial area. These powerful striking forces would then cross the Rhine and link up behind the Ruhr, thus encircling the powerhouse of the great German war machine. In the event, this did not happen, for in August 1944 the Allied forces broke out of their invasion lodgement in Normandy with such strength that their rapid thrust across France sent the German Army reeling before them. Enemy opposition collapsed everywhere to such a degree that all sectors of the line made rapid advances and were only stopped at the German border by lack of supplies. It was an exhilarating time for the pursuing troops. After being confined within a relatively small bridgehead in Normandy for so long, the open roads and demoralised enemy induced a feeling of invincibility in the Allied armies. The war seemed to be over and the Nazis beaten. But the German Army was not beaten; the Allies' pause in September 1944 allowed a few masterful generals, with experience of organised retreats on the Russian front, to re-establish the much vaunted Siegfried defensive line, reinforce and re-equip battered divisions and stabilise the front. When the advance was ready to begin again, opposition had strengthened to such an extent that Allied progress was difficult, costly and very painful. The Germans had staged a remarkable recovery.

Efforts to get momentum going again ranged from the novel to the predictable. The normally pedantic British field marshal Montgomery, who would only make a move after gaining overwhelming superiority over the enemy in troop numbers, supporting fire and logistical supplies, proposed a swift land-airborne operation to seize a lodgement over the lower Rhine at Arnhem in order to get his British 21st Army Group into northern Germany. Operation Market Garden, as it was called, was a failure, although it did establish British troops across the Maas where their lodgement could look over the border into the German Rhineland. General Bradley, commanding the US 12th Army Group, was somewhat put out when his American advance had to be delayed while men and matériel were switched northwards to help Montgomery's operation. General Patton was also irritated as supplies, especially fuel, were denied to his US 3rd Army and sent northwards. National interests came into play as British troops grabbed the headlines while Americans kicked their heels. This is where Eisenhower's 'broad front' strategy now came into play. With his armies all pressing the frontiers of the German Reich, he now believed that the war could be best won by taking territory all along the line and rolling up German forces everywhere, rather than confining the advance to small, powerful thrusts such as the Arnhem operation. It would also mean that all nationalities would be involved in the main fighting, helping to salve the national pride of the Canadian, British, American and French armies.

Farther south, Gen Bradley's US 12th Army Group spent the autumn attacking the Siegfried Line in a series of offensives, the most important and bloody of which was the capture of Aachen, where they pierced the

Supreme Allied Commander Gen Dwight D. Eisenhower (left) talks to MajGen Alvan Gillem, commander US XIII Corps (centre), and MajGen Raymond McLain, commander US XIX Corps (right). Eisenhower had previously commanded the North African 'Torch' landings and the invasions of both Sicily and Italy. (National Archives, Washington)

defensive line and got to the River Roer. In the far south, Gen Devers' US 6th Army Group had been slowed almost to a halt as they approached the German border through the difficult terrain of the Vosges Mountains. His armies became stalled by a large and troublesome pocket of German resistance at the confluence of the Saar and Moselle rivers known as the Colmar 'Pocket'. By November the deteriorating weather and enemy opposition had contrived to make any advance a slow and costly process.

Montgomery now pressed Eisenhower to modify his strategy to allow the original single major thrust through northern Germany to the Ruhr by a powerful group of British and American armies (with him at the head) to take place. Eisenhower refused and pressed on with his 'broad front', but did give permission for a combined British-American operation to clear the northern Rhineland. Montgomery's plan was to advance through his lodgement east of the River Maas, through the Reichswald and clear the enemy as far as the Rhine, while Gen Simpson's US 9th Army attacked across the River Roer and made for the Rhine. Both of these armies would then meet up and clear the whole of the Rhineland, trapping those German forces still west of the Rhine by encirclement. This operation was scheduled to start on 1 January 1945.

However, events overtook these plans when Hitler launched his Ardennes offensive on 16 December 1944. Generalfeldmarschall Gerd von Rundstedt, Commander-in-Chief West, sent his re-equipped and reconstituted 5th and 6th Panzer Armies through the lightly held Ardennes sector of the front line in Belgium, to the complete surprise of the whole of the Allied command. The battle that followed was protracted and bitter. Gains were made initially as they overran whole American divisions and caused great panic in rear areas, but the advance ran out of steam close to the River Meuse. Then the Allies set to the task of eliminating this 'bulge' in their lines. Inexorably, the great weight of their superior forces was gradually applied to the enemy's flanks, squeezing the life out of the penetration and forcing the long German retreat to begin. Within one month, they were back at their start line. Loss of life had been great on both sides; very little was achieved by the Germans. If Hitler had ever subscribed to the art of tactical defence and kept these two great panzer armies behind the Siegfried Line as a mobile reserve, instead of squandering them in the snow of the Belgian mountains, then the outcome of the final year of the war might have been a little different.

When the effects of the 'Battle of the Bulge' had finally died down, Eisenhower could once again resume his advance. Montgomery's Rhineland offensive could now go ahead with the American 9th Army led by Simpson under his command. Bradley and Devers could move their army groups to the Rhine also. All along the front line, the German Army would be squeezed back into their homeland towards complete destruction.

OPPOSING COMMANDERS

The commanders facing each other on the borders of Germany in February 1945 were each handicapped by their own philosophies. The Allied armies in the West were led by men who answered to the peoples of democratically led governments. The German army answered to one man, Adolf Hitler.

ALLIED COMMANDERS

In the Allied camp, its top commanders had achieved fame beyond the battlefield. The press and newsreels of the day portrayed them in an heroic mould, with many of them achieving the status of movie stars. Eisenhower, Montgomery, Bradley and Patton were all too famous ever to be removed from command because of their mistakes. Such changes would seriously damage morale, and more importantly, national pride. Their generalship therefore, although often questioned by politicians, Chiefs of Staff and, later, historians, was never seriously contested at the time. On the other side, German commanders were often dispatched with indecent haste by their Supreme Commander when the consequences of their actions ran counter to his expectations, even though many of them were very competent individuals.

Leading the Allied team was the Supreme Allied Commander in Europe, Gen Dwight D. Eisenhower. He was the very spirit of Allied co-operation. He was a true professional soldier of great skill with his

FM Montgomery, commander British 21st Army Group, with four Allied army commanders. From left to right: Gen Sir Miles Dempsey (British 2nd Army), LtGen Courtney Hodges (US 1st Army), Montgomery, LtGen Bill Simpson (US 9th Army) and Gen Harry Crerar (Canadian 1st Army). (National Archives, Washington)

most prominent asset being his ability as an administrator, rather than as a great strategist. His role was to weld together the vast armies of American, British, Canadian, Polish, French and Belgian troops into a powerful fighting force. That he achieved this, in spite of the efforts of his strong-willed and often troublesome subordinate commanders, is a testament to his diplomatic and people skills. Eisenhower may have lacked experience as a field commander, but his mastery of the technicalities of war, his exceptional logistical gifts and his exercise of tact and diplomacy, enabled him to achieve all that was expected of him.

Eisenhower's Army Group Commanders lined up along the German frontier were, from north to south, Montgomery, Bradley and Devers; one British and two American. Field Marshal Bernard Montgomery commanded the British 21st Army Group, comprising Canadian 1st Army, British 2nd Army and US 9th Army, with great success. He began the war as a divisional commander, shot to fame with his handling of 8th Army in North Africa and, with command of all land forces during the D-Day landings, became the most prominent British field commander of the war. He was the master of the 'set-piece' battle. Careful planning, calculated strategy and disciplined use of all logistical supplies, marked his approach to warfare. He never acted until he had overwhelming superiority over his enemy in both men and matériel. He showed unconcealed scorn for those commanders who relied on fortune and élan to carry them through. Montgomery was a showman able to exploit media interest at home and inspire great confidence in his men in the field. He was generally disliked by his American allies; his abrasive manner and nationalistic approach to the conduct of the war also irritated many of his contemporaries.

General Omar Bradley was America's counterpart to Montgomery, commanding the massive US 12th Army Group which, in February 1945, consisted of the US 1st and 3rd Armies (Bradley's US 9th Army was on loan to Montgomery for the Rhineland campaign). Bradley was the most important US field general of the war. In 1942, during the 'Torch' invasion of North Africa, he acted in a liaison role for Eisenhower, later commanding a corps at the end of the campaign. Service in Sicily, in a subordinate command to Gen Patton, followed. He was eventually given the US 1st Army for the Normandy invasion. By 1 August he had risen to army group command with almost one-and-a-half million American troops under his control–the largest army ever assembled under the command of a single American general. Bradley had a quiet and unassuming manner, a great respect for his men and a sure grasp of strategy and tactics. His relationship with Eisenhower was one of mutual respect, for although he lacked the flair and drive of Gen Patton, his performance was solid, dependable and effective.

The last of Eisenhower's army group commanders, at the head of US 6th Army Group, was LtGen Jacob Devers. The least well known of all the major commanders, Devers had approached the German border from the south via the landings on the French Riviera. His army group comprised US 7th Army and the French 1st Army. Devers had started the war in charge of a division and by 1943 was in command of all American forces in the UK. He went to the Mediterranean as deputy to the Supreme Allied Commander, Gen Henry Maitland Wilson, and gained experience there of handling large formations. Devers was later selected to head the invasion of southern France. His army group's progress from the Mediterranean had been relatively easy compared to that faced by other Allied units in Normandy, with major enemy opposition only increasing as he approached the German border.

Making up these three army groups were a clutch of army commanders whose performances ranged from the pedantic to the outrageous. In the extreme north Canadian 1st Army had LtGen Henry Crerar at its head. By nature a reserved man, he hated personal publicity. He was also handicapped, not only by having Montgomery as his boss, but by being required to report daily to the Canadian Prime Minister, Mackenzie King, and ultimately to the Canadian Parliament. He suffered by having two masters; his every move was scrutinised directly both by politicians and his army group commander. None the less, his great skill in handling the logistical side of the 'Veritable' campaign and his cool nerves in mastering the largest force ever commanded by a Canadian general – over 475,000 men – more than made up for his cool relationship with Monty.

Heading British 2nd Army was LtGen Miles Dempsey, another very modest general who shied publicity. His role in the Rhineland campaign was secondary as his forces were being kept back for the Rhine Crossing. Mongomery's third army commander was the American LtGen Bill Simpson, whose US 9th Army would handle the southern part of Montgomery's Rhineland operation. Simpson's army was the youngest of them all, having joined the campaign in north-west Europe towards the end of 1944. Tall, bald, amiable, Simpson was a good subordinate to both Montgomery and Bradley, keeping himself above politics and personalities, being content to fight his army to the best of his ability, no matter whom he reported to.

Bradley's army commanders presented two contrasting styles. At the head of the US 1st Army was LtGen Courtney Hodges, who had taken over the formation when Bradley was promoted to army group commander. Hodges had been Bradley's deputy and understudy and slipped into the command of 1st Army with ease, continuing to fight the army in the mould of Bradley: cautious, dependable and thorough. In complete contrast was LtGen George Patton with his US 3rd Army. 'Old Blood and Guts' Patton was certainly the exception of all the major Allied generals. A cavalry man, he was an outstanding practitioner of mobile warfare, believing in employing bold tactics and always being on the offensive. Patton commanded a corps in North Africa and Sicily, and came close to being returned to the USA as a result of his forceful and bullying manner. Eisenhower gave him a chance to redeem himself with the 3rd Army in north-west Europe and his successful performance and wide sweeping thrusts into the German-occupied territory made him immensely popular with the American press. His tactics of pushing forward at any cost certainly caused unease in the enemy camp. Many German commanders considered Patton to be the best of the Allied generals.

The US 7th Army, commanded by LtGen Alexander Patch, was part of Devers' 6th Army Group. Patch had arrived in the European theatre after successfully commanding US forces against the Japanese at Guadalcanal in the Pacific. Together with the French 1st Army under Gen Jean de Lattre de Tassigny, the US 7th Army landed along the coast of southern France in August 1944 and advanced up the Rhone valley in pursuit of the German 19th Army.

GERMAN COMMANDERS

At the head of the German army was Adolf Hitler. He exercised total command over every strategic decision. By 1945 his health had deteriorated and he was a broken man, yet he still kept a very tight hold on the German conduct of the war. As a result, every major decision, and many minor ones, had to be agreed by him. His main strategy at that point was that Germany was to be defended at all costs and the Rhine was to remain inviolate: there was to be no retreat. It mattered little that tactics might demand a realignment of the front, his generals made such withdrawals at their peril. His contribution to the campaign was negative and ultimately aided the Allies more than his own side. Hitler's greatest mistake was to force his generals to squander their strength in front of the Rhine, rather than to get behind the river and use the obstacle as a defensive moat, where his mobile reserves could pinch off any attempted crossing.

At the head of the German forces facing the Allies was GFM Gerd von Rundstedt, Commander-in-Chief West. One of the old school of professional German soldiers, Von Rundstedt commanded army groups during the campaigns in Poland in 1939 and France in 1940. After the victory in France he was promoted to field marshal and commanded Army Group South during the invasion of Russia. He was sacked by Hitler for staging a tactical retreat at Rostov, but was later reinstated to take over Army Group West in France in order to head off the likely Allied invasion. After the July Plot of 1944 he was again dismissed by Hitler, only to be restored to command once again in the West prior to the Ardennes offensive. He was one of the most offensive-minded of the German generals, but by 1945 had realised that the war was lost and could only be prolonged by withdrawing behind the Rhine.

Confronting the Allies along the German border Von Rundstedt had lined up Army Groups H, B and G. At the head of Army Group H, having taken over the formation early in February 1945, was GenObst Johannes Blaskowitz, a veteran commander of armies in Poland and Russia. Blaskowitz was one of the most senior German generals but blighted his career when he ran foul of Hitler with his criticism of the SS in occupied Poland. A professional of the old school like Von Rundstedt, Blaskowitz soldiered on from an obstinate sense of duty. Even though he was discredited by his leader, his professional pride remained intact and he fought his army with all the power that was available.

The commander of Army Group B was, in great contrast to Blaskowitz and Von Rundstedt, a confirmed Nazi. Generalfeldmarshall Walther Model was a favourite general of Hitler's who had risen to fame through his exploits in Russia, being promoted from command of a division to army commander within months. Model was regarded as being one of the major defensive strategists of the war. His handling of army groups during the retreat in Russia and the stabilisation of the Western Front in the autumn of 1944, helped preserve the strength of the dwindling German army. He was on the spot during the Arnhem operation and was able to organise the local units swiftly in order to contain the British attack. Against his better judgement he was ordered to carry out the ill-fated Ardennes offensive and could not be blamed for its failure. Model was one of the best of the younger generation of generals.

GenObst Johannes Blaskowitz, Commander Army Group H, was an infantryman of the old school and one of the most senior German generals. He commanded the German 8th Army in the war against Poland and was later head of the army of occupation there. It was in Poland that he became appalled at the conduct of the SS and sent a note about their conduct to Brauchitsch and Jodl. Hitler got to hear of it and the incident blighted Blaskowitz's career. He was passed over during the grand promotions of 1940, when many generals junior to him were elevated to field marshal. He was not given another fighting command for the next four years until after the Allies landed in Normandy in 1944. (Imperial War Museum)

Commanding Army Group G was GenObst der Waffen-SS Paul Hausser. Another veteran of the old Imperial Army, Hausser retired as a lieutenant general in 1932 but came back into service in 1934 in order to organise the training of the Waffen SS. He gave good account of himself later in the war during the fighting in Russia in command of the SS Panzer Corps at Kursk. He led the II SS Panzer Corps in France against the British and later became the first SS officer ever to command an army when he took over the German 7th Army.

Lined up along the German border facing the Allies were six German armies: 1st Parachute Army, 15th Army, 5th Panzer Army, 7th Army, 1st Army and 19th Army. Commanding the 1st Parachute Army was Gen der Fallschirmtruppen Alfred Schlemm, a veteran with an outstanding fighting record. A divisional field commander in Russia, Schlemm became Student's Chief of Staff in Crete. He was then given I Parachute Corps in Italy. He stoutly defended the Anzio perimeter after the Allied landings and then performed a series of remarkable defensive actions during the retreat up the Italian mainland.

The German 15th Army had Gen der Infanterie Gustav von Zangen at its head. General von Zangen commanded the 17th Infantry Division in Russia in 1942, a corps in France during 1943 and an army detachment in Italy before he moved into the command of 15th Army on the Western Front. General der Panzertruppen Hasso von Manteuffel was in command of 5th Panzer Army. Manteuffel had led Rommel's old 7th Panzer Division in Russia, and was at the head of the 5th Panzer Army during the Ardennes campaign. Another army commander who had been present during Hitler's winter offensive was Gen der Panzertruppen Erich Brandenberger. He still commanded the 7th Army opposite the Americans and had previously led the 8th Panzer Division during the invasion of Russia. Holding the far south of the line, opposite the American 6th Army Group on the upper Rhine, were the German 1st and 19th Armies. The 1st Army was led by Gen der Infanterie Hermann Foertsch, and the German 19th Army was commanded by Gen der Panzertruppen Hermann Balck.

GFM Walther Model, Commander Army Group B, was a confirmed Nazi and one of Hitler's favourite generals. After a successful period in Russia where he rose from head of the 3rd Panzer Division to the command of both Army Group North Ukraine and Army Group Centre, he was recalled to the West to take over Army Group B in France. In December 1944 he undertook Hitler's Ardennes offensive, although he had grave doubts about its objectives. Model was one of the best of the German field generals; he had a great ability as a defence strategist and a sound understanding of the tactics of tank warfare. (Imperial War Museum)

OPPOSING ARMIES

The collapse of the Ardennes offensive in 1945 had left the German Army with an even greater sense of despair than it had felt when the Allies had first arrived at the Reich border. Morale was low; units were dramatically under strength, equipment was poorly maintained and new supplies were meagre, and spasmodic. A fanatical determination still prevailed throughout the forces, but each man knew that the war was almost certainly lost. There was nothing to fight for but the homeland. It was, however, a homeland that was being overrun, not only by the British and Americans, but by an even more terrifying horde from the East: the Russians had begun their new winter campaign and were pressing towards Berlin.

On paper the German forces facing the Allies along the Rhineland and down to the Swiss border still seemed formidable and quite comparable to those of their enemies. Commander-in-Chief West, Gerd von Rundstedt, in principle, controlled nearly 60 divisions. However, most of these German units had become just a pale shadow of their former strength and effectiveness, while the Allies' forces were still remarkably intact, albeit nominally under strength through earlier heavy fighting and reduced numbers of reinforcements. In western Europe Eisenhower had at his disposal 3 army groups, 9 armies, 20 corps and 73 divisions of which 49 were infantry, 20 armoured and 4 airborne. However, not all of these units were on the Western Front. Over three million Allied soldiers had been shipped into the war zone since June 1944. Great as the battles on the Western Front were, Germany had a

Exhausted German infantry captured by the Americans during their drive to the Rhine. The picture shows the desperate plight of the German Army at that time, with much of its number made up of old men and youths. (National Archives, Washington)

LEFT Troops of the 1st Battalion, 120th Regiment, from the US 30th Division near Wesel, in pursuit of the retreating 116th Panzer Division, during US 9th Army's drive to the River Rhine. The infantry are supported by an M24 'Chaffee' light tank, carrying a .3 inch (75mm) M6 gun. (National Archives, Washington)

Troops of the 15th Scottish Division dug in on the side of the road in front of Cleve. These men of the Argyll and Sutherland Highlanders were consolidating the gains made during the first two days of the Reichswald battle, before launching their attack on the town. (Imperial War Museum)

much bigger adversary to deal with to the east. Facing the Russians Hitler had 133 German divisions and, in addition to this, there were 24 German divisions in Italy, 17 in Scandinavia and 10 in Yugoslavia.

The German Army of early 1945 was markedly different from the all-conquering legions that spread out across Europe at the beginning of the conflict. The great losses sustained during the drawn-out campaigns in Russia – on a scale and ferocity that dwarfed that of all other theatres of war – had crippled the German Army. Reinforcements had to be gleaned from a variety of sources, including enlisting Russian and east European prisoners. All this diluted the 'racial purity' of the original army and led to a sharp decline in standards. Fitness ideals had been relaxed and those with definite physical problems, such as loss of hearing and stomach ulcers, had been admitted into fighting units. Many of the German divisions had been raised on a reduced scale, with only two infantry regiments, instead of three, each containing only two infantry and two artillery battalions, instead of three. In contrast, Allied divisions were raised with a full complement of men, equipment, transport and support. The great manufacturing power of the major Allied nations ensured that this was so.

In manpower terms both sides were having to dig deep to provide reinforcements. The British were the most sorely pressed, having had to resort to disbanding units to provide replacements for the fighting divisions. The USA was also under serious pressure having to deal with competing claims for new divisions not only from western Europe, but from those armies fighting in the Italian and Pacific theatres; they also wanted new blood. In late January there were only six divisions left in the USA that had been scheduled to be sent overseas, four of which were

Infantry from US 9th Division watch a demonstration, early in February 1945, of the use of a 2.36 inch (660mm) anti-tank rocket launcher M9A1–the bazooka. The M9A1 fired a 3.4lb (1.53kg) hollow charge rocket and had a maximum range of 400 yards (364m). Almost half-a-million bazookas were built during the war. (National Archives, Washington)

earmarked for Europe. However, the Germans still had reserves on which to draw, for in January 1945 Hitler decreed that older men up to 45 years of age should be shifted from industry to the armed forces. In February eight new divisions were created, many of them made up of youths just turned 17. So fanatical was their indoctrination, the Germans were able to convert these raw recruits into dangerous and effective defenders in just a few weeks.

The individual soldier fighting for the Allies was well fed, well equipped and well clothed compared to his German opponent. The large supply train that led back across Europe to the sea shipped forward, right to the front line, vast amounts of stores providing for all his needs and a great many of his comforts. The quantity and quality of the supplies sustaining the Allied armies in the field could only be dreamed of by the Germans. In almost every measure, the Allies were superior to their enemy: in numerical terms, they had three times the artillery, ten times the number of tanks, four times the aircraft and two-and-a-half times the number of troops. Their superiority in the design of battle-worthy equipment was not so apparent, with the Germans having two world-beating tanks, the Panther and the Tiger, an excellent multipurpose artillery piece, the notable 0.34 inch (88mm) and very effective lower calibre infantry weapons such as the MG42 and Panzerfaust. The standard Allied tank, the Sherman, was no match head-to-head with the German main battle tank, but it was present on the battlefield in such numbers that it was always the most effective. The British 25-pdr (11.25kg) field gun, supporting every divisional attack, was probably the best in the world.

In the air, the German Luftwaffe still had a large number of aircraft – over 5,000 operational in November 1944 – but was really a spent force. It did manage to put over 1,000 planes into the air on New Year's Day 1945 over northern France, Belgium and The Netherlands, in support of the Ardennes offensive, but the effort proved to be a last show of strength that could never again be repeated. A shortage of trained pilots and difficulties in the supply of aviation fuel grounded all but a few sporadic fighter bombers carrying out hit-and-run attacks. In contrast, the Allies could muster a tremendously powerful air armada. In close support of ground troops were six tactical air commands. The British 2nd Tactical Air Force supported the British and Canadians, whilst the 1st French Air Corps aided the French 1st Army. The Americans had the IX, XI, XIX and XXIX Tactical Air Commands providing support for the US 1st, 7th, 3rd and 9th Armies. All of this was backed by 11 groups of medium and light bombers of the IX US Bomber Command. And behind all this were the mighty US Eighth Air Force and the fighters and bombers of the Royal Air Force; in total 17,500 first-line combat aircraft could be called upon to harass the enemy.

The reality of defeat that permeated the German Army in 1945 dictated that its strategy would have to be one of defence. It had once been the best offensive army that the world has ever seen, but events had overtaken the army of the 'Blitzkrieg' and it now had to employ the same tactics that it had derided its British and French enemies for practising during the glory days of 1940. The initiative is always in the hands of the attacker and it was hard for the Germans to have to react to the moves of its enemies, rather than to order the flow of the battle for themselves. Their goals and options were now simply to try to survive, just like the British did in 1940.

American troops from 102nd Division, US XIII Corps, raid German houses in Lovenich looking for mattresses with which to line their foxholes. Although looting was officially frowned upon, nothing could stop the infantryman acquiring anything that made his spartan life a little more comfortable. (National Archives, Washington)

OPPOSING PLANS

In late January Eisenhower presented his ideas for the further prosecution of the war. Although still maintaining his 'broad front' strategy with his first intention being to destroy the main elements of the German Army west of the Rhine and then to develop mobile operations east of the river, his main emphasis was to engineer the elimination of the great manufacturing area of the Ruhr. The thrust of the Allied advance would then be north-east through the north German Plain. This more or less consigned the decisive battle of the Rhineland to 21st Army Group since it was the nearest group to the Ruhr industrial area.

Eisenhower knew that when Montgomery launched his proposed attack south-east from the Nijmegen area through the narrow passage between the Maas and the Rhine, he would be attacking one of the most heavily fortified sectors of the Siegfried Line. This was the shortest route to the Ruhr, and Hitler knew it. The region was of such importance to the German war effort that any attempt to capture it was bound to provoke a desperate German reaction. Although Hitler had laid down that every metre of German soil was to be defended to the last, some parts had to be defended more than others. This was one of those sectors. Operation Veritable, as the attack was called, was sure to develop into a very costly and difficult one.

A Churchill bridging tank is brought forward through the Reichswald to tackle an anti-tank ditch. In the background is another Churchill with a fascine strapped to its front, ready to drop it into a stream or gully to provide a crossing place for armour. These ready-made bridges and fascines often rendered anti-tank defences immediately obsolete by enabling a crossing to be made of the obstacle within minutes. (Imperial War Museum)

A mortar team from 2nd Battalion Middlesex Regiment fires its 4.2 inch (107mm) mortar in support of the British 3rd Division during the attack on Kervenheim. The 4.2 inch (107mm) mortar was one of the heavy infantry weapons provided by a machine gun battalion to each infantry division. The Middlesex Regiment supplied heavy machine-guns and mortars via the four of its battalions who were attached to the 3rd, 15th, 43rd and 51st Infantry Divisions throughout the war in north-west Europe. (Imperial War Museum)

To help 21st Army Group succeed with 'Veritable' Eisenhower had given Montgomery one of Bradley's armies – Gen Simpson's US 9th Army – from US 12th Army Group. Simpson's forces would attack across the River Roer 60 miles (96km) to the south two days after the launching of 'Veritable', and then turn north to link up with Montgomery and help clear the way to the Rhine opposite the Ruhr. The combined armies would then launch an assault over the Rhine, once all the Allied forces had gained the west bank along its complete length, in order to encircle the great industrial area. The US 9th Army's attack across the Roer and subsequent advance was given the code name 'Grenade'.

While this great attack was taking place in the north, Eisenhower's other forces would continue to push back the enemy in front of the Rhine. Bradley's other two armies, the 1st and the 3rd, were faced by ground that was not suitable for mobile warfare, so the advance was planned to develop in stages. First the heavily forested high ground of the Eifel had to be cleared, then, to the south, the triangle of land between the confluence of the Saar and Moselle rivers had to be captured to bring Patton's 3rd Army up to the main fortifications of the Siegfried Line. But perhaps the most important immediate objective of US 1st Army, was the capture of the Roer dams. The seven dams controlled the flow of water along the River Roer in front of Simpson's US 9th Army. They were capable of flooding the whole of the low ground alongside the Roer producing a formidable water barrier should the Germans choose to destroy them. With the dams in German hands, Simpson could not attack across the river for fear of his rear being cut off by this rising water. The dams had to be captured before 'Grenade' could go ahead. They were, however, a formidable objective. The Americans had been trying to capture them (albeit often in a half-hearted way) since 15 December. Bradley was now told to redouble his efforts and seize them.

Next to Bradley's army group, to the south, was Devers' 6th Army Group. Devers had already reached the Rhine south of Strasbourg, but the Germans still had an expansive bridgehead, measuring 30 by 50 miles, (48 by 80km) on the west bank around the town of Colmar, known to the Allies as the Colmar 'Pocket'. Eliminating this bridgehead was essential to Eisenhower's plans to build a complete line along the Rhine before attempting any crossings of the river. The elimination of this pocket was begun in the final weeks of January by one American and five French divisions of Gen Jean de Lattre de Tassigny's French 1st Army.

The main handicap facing Von Rundstedt and his generals was Hitler's long-standing decree forbidding any voluntary withdrawal. With the bulk of the Siegfried defensive line still intact, Hitler felt that his policy of 'hold till the last' could be implemented by his troops. Not a

American infantry from 334th Infantry Regiment, inspecting a German 4.75 inch (122mm) schwere Feldhaubitze being used in an anti-tank role. The howitzer, a captured Russian artillery piece, had been in service with the Red Army since 1938 and was one of the most successful and reliable guns of the war. This particular gun had been captured on 1 March in a surprise night attack on the town of Boisheim by the US 84th Division, where the 334th's 3rd Battalion caught the whole garrison asleep. Eight of these guns covered the approaches to the town, but none had been manned during the night. (National Archives, Washington)

defensive bunker or pillbox was to be relinquished wittingly; each had to be prised from the defenders at great cost to the attackers. Hitler also delayed granting authority for preparing other defensive positions to the rear, fearing that these new fortifications would act as a fall-back zone of refuge to the forward troops and encourage retreat into them. The German Army would have to stand its ground and absorb the shock of the attack as best it could. It had already demonstrated an adeptness to soak up punishment; it would now have to exercise its proven ability to improvise, block, mend, and delay, just as it had done during the two preceding years in North Africa, Italy, France and Russia.

The German forces facing the Allies west of the Rhine were very thinly spread. They were, however, along much of their front, ensconced inside the fortifications of the Siegfried Line. Unfortunately for the Germans, this line was not as strong as Nazi propaganda had made out, as it had never been properly completed along its whole length, nor did it have the weapons and manpower that it was designed to have. If the strategy for which it had been planned had been implemented – fixed fortifications equipped with their full complement of men and guns, and with a mobile armoured reserve behind the line able to attack any Allied penetration – then the battles to clear the Rhineland might have been more equally balanced. As it was, there were just too few troops to deal with all the attacks along the front.

Von Rundstedt's three army groups barred the way into the Reich: in the north was Army Group H (Blaskowitz), in the middle Army Group B

(Model) and in the south was Army Group G (Hausser). Generaloberst Johannes Blaskowitz had control of two armies: the XXV Army (Von Blumentritt) in Holland which did not take part in the Rhineland battles and the I Parachute Army (Schlemm) holding the line inside Germany west of the Rhine from the ground opposite Nijmegen in the north to Roermond on the River Maas in the south, the ground over which the 'Veritable' and 'Grenade' offensives would strike. General der Fallschirmtruppen Alfred Schlemm's army consisted of four corps, three in the line and one as a mobile reserve. The bulk of these forces were in the northern sector covering the Rhine approaches, with the line most lightly held in the south opposite Venlo and Roermond. Schlemm was keeping his armour in a central position behind a weaker screen of infantrymen.

Generalfeldmarshall Walther Model, commander Army Group B, held the line opposite Bradley's American forces. Model knew that some American units had been shifted to the north and felt that the main American thrust would come in the area of Roermond, with the British 2nd Army attacking across the River Maas near Venlo. He also thought that Bradley would press on with his advance through the Eifel, continuing the moves that he had performed so well in clearing the last of the 'Bulge'. Model's forces consisted of XV Army (Von Zangen) in the North, V Panzer Army (Manteuffel) holding the centre and VII Army (Brandenberger) opposite Patton's US 3rd Army in the south.

Generaloberst der Waffen SS Paul Hausser, commander Army Group G, was using his armies to oppose LtGen Patch's US 7th Army Group. Hausser had two armies of his own: 1st Army (Foertsch) and 19th Army (Balck) to hold the Siegfried Line around Saarbrücken and the eastern banks of the southern Rhine.

The opposing sides then were lined up for a fight: the Allies in attack and the Germans in defence. Both sides knew that the key to the coming offensives was in the north, with the Germans not knowing exactly where the blow would fall, but having a good idea that it would be aimed at an early crossing of the Rhine and the capture of the Ruhr industrial area.

OPERATION VERITABLE

Field Marshal Montgomery had decided that 'Veritable' was to be planned and executed by Canadian 1st Army, under the command of LtGen Henry Crerar. The battle was to be the largest Allied offensive since Normandy. Crerar was to deploy his men along the front line south-east of Nijmegen close to the German border and to attack through the corridor between the Rhine and Maas rivers. Barring the way along this proposed route was the dense forest of the Reichswald, with just a small strip of land on either side available for forward movement: to the north the open land was barely a mile wide and bounded by the flooded River Rhine; to the south it was confined by the flooded Maas. Running across the path of the advance was one of the most difficult sections of the Siegfried Line's fortifications. Crerar's objective was to break through this defensive line and then unleash his armoured troops into the flat area of the Rhineland, heading south to meet up with the Americans and south-eastwards to seize the east bank of the Rhine. At this point the British 2nd Army (Dempsey) would join in the battle, crossing the Maas unopposed into areas already captured by Canadian 1st Army.

Crerar employed five divisions for the initial breakthrough: two Canadian divisions from Canadian II Corps (Simonds), the 2nd and 3rd Infantry Divisions, and three divisions from British XXX Corps (Horrocks), the 15th Scottish, 51st Highland and 53rd Welsh Divisions. The commander of Canadian 1st Army planned for two divisions to attack into the Reichswald (British 51st and 53rd Divisions) while two other divisions (Canadian 2nd and British 15th Divisions) provided flank

This scene of troops moving over frozen ground was taken on 21 January, 18 days before the start of 'Veritable'. During the planning stages of the operation, it was hoped to make the attack over frozen ground so that tanks could advance with the infantry and wheeled traffic could move freely. The thaw that set in just a few days before the start of 'Veritable' resulted in a battle that was handicapped by the mud almost as much as by the enemy. (Imperial War Museum)

Commander British 21st Army Group, FM Montgomery, with the men who ran 'Veritable'. From left to right: MajGen C. Vokes (Canadian 4th Armored Division), Gen Harry Crerar (Canadian 1st Army), Montgomery, LtGen Brian Horrocks (British XXX Corps), LtGen G. Simonds (Canadian II Corps), MajGen Dan Spry (Canadian 3rd Division) and MajGen A. Matthews (Canadian 2nd Division).
(Imperial War Museum)

BELOW Dead German infantryman of the 84th Division killed during the shelling at the start of 'Veritable' on 8 February. The man lies in a communication trench on the edge of the Reichswald which had been captured by the 5th/7th Gordon Highlanders, part of 51st Highland Division.
(Imperial War Museum)

protection outside of the forest to the north. The fifth division (Canadian 3rd Division) was to become waterborne and clear the enemy from the isolated fortified villages which had become stranded by the rising floodwaters, but whose artillery still constituted a sideways threat to those troops outside of the forest. All of the divisions were placed under the immediate command of LtGen Brian Horrocks of British XXX Corps. Once the breakthrough had been accomplished, the British 43rd Wessex Division and the Guards Armoured Division would be introduced into the battle with the intention of securing the line Gennep–Asperden–Cleve. This was the final objective of 'Veritable', from then on the battlefield would open out and a more mobile warfare would take place, albeit still within the confines of an area littered with extemporised fortifications, the most notable of which was the 'Hochwald Layback' which covered the approaches to Xanten and the Rhine bridges at Wesel.

A complicated deception plan had been engineered by the Canadians to mislead the enemy as to the location of the forthcoming attack. Road and radio traffic was increased to the west of Nijmegen along the River Waal and lower River Maas, to give the impression that the troops there were being reinforced in preparation for an attack northwards into Holland, towards Utrecht and Amsterdam. The actual build-up of forces opposite the Reichswald was prepared silently and with great ingenuity without alerting the Germans. When the offensive was finally launched, it was able to achieve total surprise to most of the German high command.

General Schlemm, however, believed that the Allies would take advantage of their presence over the River Maas near Nijmegen and launch an attack through the Reichswald. Blaskowitz would have none of it, for he was convinced that the attack would happen much farther south and refused Schlemm permission to move any extra troops northwards to strengthen the Reichswald area. None the less, Schlemm did slip three battalions of first-class paratroopers from 2nd Parachute Regiment (Lackner) into the forest to help bolster the defences of Gen Fiebig's 84th Infantry Division who were holding the line there.

25

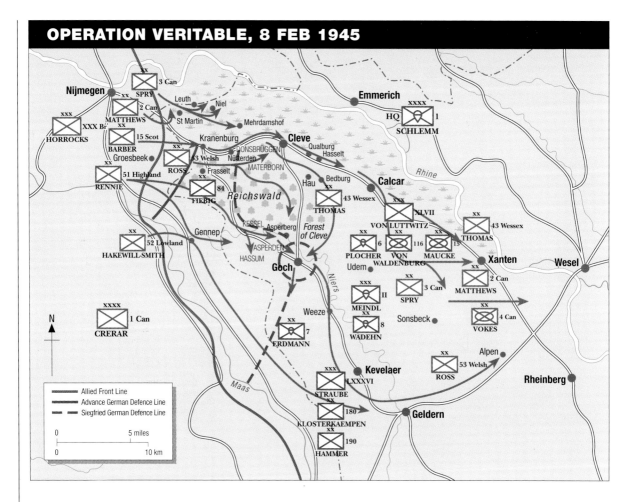

Allied intelligence had shown that in the northern area facing the Canadians there would be the three corps of Schlemm's 1st Parachute Army. Holding the line from the Rhine to Udem, but held back as the Wehrmacht's only mobile reserve, was the German XLVII Corps of Gen der Panzertruppen Heinrich Freiherr von Luttwitz, consisting of 6th Parachute Division (Plocher), 116th Panzer Division (Von Waldenburg) and the 15th Panzer Grenadiers (Maucke). From Udem to Weeze was II Parachute Corps commanded by GenLt Eugen Meindl with 7th Parachute Division (Erdmann), 8th Parachute Division (Wadehn) and 84th Infantry Division (Fiebig) under his control. General der Infanterie Erich Straube commanded the LXXXVI Corps who were responsible for the line from the south of Weeze to the south of Venlo. The corps comprised 180th Infantry Division (Klosterkemper) and 190th Infantry Division (Hammer).

Many of Schlemm's formations were not at the front but were held back from the line, waiting for any Allied penetration. The whole scheme of the Siegfried Line was that its forward outer line was held by light troops whose purpose was to slow down the attack for long enough for reinforcements to be rushed into the contested area to man the main second-line defences. Thus, although the Reichswald front itself was held by only one division, the 84th, Gen Schlemm could get two parachute, one panzer, and one panzer grenadier divisions to its aid within a day.

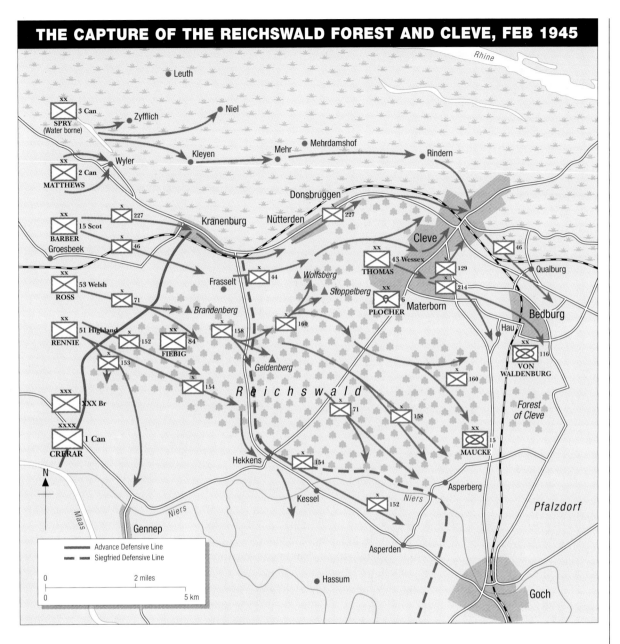

During the planning stages of 'Veritable', Gen Crerar knew that there would be two great questions hanging over the battle. The first concerned the weather. The winter of 1944/45 had been harsh and much of the planning had taken place with a background of frequent snow falls and hard frosts. The ground in northern Germany was frozen solid. This was perfect for operations, but if the weather thawed and the terrain turned to mud, the offensive would be severely hampered. In the event the cold weather did not hold; a rise in temperature a few days before the start of the operation, and the onslaught of heavy rains, turned the battlefield into a quagmire. In delaying the start of the offensive until early February, the advantage provided by the cold frozen ground was lost.

The other worrying question concerned the attack by Simpson's 9th Army. His assault across the River Roer – Operation Grenade – was

British troops from 5th/7th Argyll and Sutherland Highlanders of 15th Scottish Division cross the border from Holland into Germany on the first day of 'Veritable'. The shell-torn house and barbed-wire fence mark the boundary of German territory. (Imperial War Museum)

scheduled to take place two days after the launch of 'Veritable', just long enough later to throw the Germans off balance. But there could be no crossing of the river until the Roer dams had been captured by US 1st Army and the threat of flooding removed. Simpson could not afford to have the rear of his army cut off from its supply base by rising water. Would the dams be captured in time? It was important that the two offensives be mutually supporting, for if Simpson could not attack, then Montgomery's forces would draw German reinforcements onto their front which would make for a very difficult fight indeed.

Operation Veritable got underway on 8 February, heralded by a night-time bomber raid on Cleve and Goch in which both towns were completely destroyed. Further raids on Emmerich, Calcar, Udem and Weeze contributed to the disruption of enemy communications. As soon as the last bomber headed for home the massed artillery began their bombardment of preselected targets in the path of the Canadian advance, firing the heaviest barrage employed by the British during the war. These guns were later joined by the aimed fire of tanks, anti-tank guns, rocket projectors, mortars and machine guns, concentrating on

Artillerymen from the Canadian 3rd Division dig in after having moved up their 25pdr guns. Two days into the 'Veritable' battle, the Canadians were due to support the Scottish Division in their attack on Cleve. (Imperial War Museum)

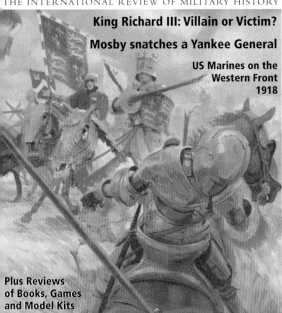

OSPREY

MILITARY JOURNAL

THE INTERNATIONAL REVIEW OF MILITARY HISTORY

King Richard III: Villain or Victim?

Mosby snatches a Yankee General

US Marines on the Western Front 1918

Plus Reviews of Books, Games and Model Kits

Fascinating articles on military history from antiquity to modern times

The Wars of the Roses
Terence Wise
Illustrated by Gerry Embleton

CAMPAIGN 69
NAGASHINO 1575
SLAUGHTER AT THE BARRICADES
STEPHEN TURNBULL

OSPREY AIRCRAFT OF THE ACES 30
French Aces of World War 2
Barry Ketley

WARRIOR SERIES 16
BRITISH TOMMY
1914–18
WEAPONS · ARMOUR · TACTICS
MARTIN PEGLER · MIKE CHAPPELL

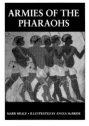

ARMIES OF THE PHARAOHS
MARK HEALY · ILLUSTRATED BY ANGUS McBRIDE

NEW VANGUARD 33
M3 & M5 STUART LIGHT TANK
1940–1945
STEVEN J. ZALOGA · JIM LAURIER

THE SAMURAI
ANTHONY J BRYANT ILLUSTRATED BY ANGUS McBRIDE

MEN-AT-ARMS 339
THE KING'S GERMAN LEGION (2) 1812–1816
MIKE CHAPPELL

TEXAS RANGERS
DR STEPHEN HARDIN
ILLUSTRATED BY RICHARD HOOK

RENOWNED FOR OVER 30 YEARS
Visit Osprey at www.ospreypublishing.com

OSPREY MILITARY JOURNAL - From the world's leading publisher of illustrated military history. Bi monthly (six issues per year) 64 pages per issue fully illustrated in Osprey's unique style with artwork, maps, charts and photos. Fascinating articles on military history from ancient times to the present day and expert guidance for enthusiasts.

☐
(Please tick)
Please send me full details of the Osprey Military Journal, with no obligation to subscribe.

☐
(Please tick)
Please send me regular information about Osprey books.

Primary area of interest:

☐ History ☐ Aviation ☐ Modelling ☐ Wargaming
(Please tick)   (Please tick)   (Please tick)   (Please tick)

other...

Title/Rank (*BLOCK LETTERS PLEASE*) First name: _____

Last name: _____

Address: _____

_____

_____

Postcode/Zip: _____ Country: _____

Tel: _____ E-mail address: _____

The publisher may wish to pass on your details to carefully selected companies with publications or products of possible interest to you. If you prefer not to receive such offers, please tick here ☐

MAIL/FAX THIS CARD TO

In **UK, Europe and other countries**

Osprey Direct
PO Box 140
Wellingborough
Northants
NN8 4ZA
UK

Tel +44 (0)1933 443863
Fax +44 (0)1933 443849
or E-mail info@ospreydirect.co.uk

In **USA and Canada**

Osprey Direct USA
PO Box 130
Sterling Heights
MI 48311-0130
USA

Tel (810) 795-2763
Fax (810) 795-4266
or E-mail info@ospreydirectusa.com

Visit Osprey at www.ospreypublishing.com

targets close to the start line. After five-and-a-half hours' continuous fire, the barrage began to lift and the infantry moved forward.

Facing the troops as they advanced across the open ground were the outer layers of the Siegfried Line, Hitler's great Westwall. These outpost positions consisted of extensive minefields followed by a double line of trenches protected by an anti-tank ditch, just in front of the Reichswald. Every farmhouse and village near the forest had been converted into a strong-point, with reinforced cellars and gun emplacements built into them. These makeshift bunkers were all interconnected with communication trenches stretching back into the woods. Roads were blocked with concrete and steel obstacles, covered by anti-tank guns. Three miles (4.8km) further into the Reichswald were the main defence lines, with concrete pillboxes and reinforced bunkers, barbed-wire entanglements, tank traps and emplaced guns. The lines ran through the forest from north to south and extended beyond the limits of the woods, linking up with the flooded Rhine and Maas rivers, completely barring any passage. Spurs of these lines connected up to the fortified towns of Cleve and Goch creating an area of almost impenetrable fortifications. Manning the defences were the German 84th Infantry Division, commanded by GenMaj Heinz Fiebig. The division consisted of about 10,000 men, but contained many substandard units including men grouped together with specific health problems such as the 'Magen' battalion of men with stomach problems, and the 'Ohren' battalion of troops with poor hearing. Volkssturm units, made up of local men aged from 16 to 60 who were capable of bearing arms, were also present in the division. The brutal fact was that these troops were expendable, manning defences which would inevitably crumple under the weight of an Allied attack, but which would delay the advance long enough for seasoned troops to be brought into the line.

The Canadian attack began with four divisions at 1030hrs, when the artillery barrage lifted and rolled forward in front of the advancing troops. The Canadian 2nd Division, commanded by MajGen A. B. Matthews, attacked on the extreme left flank of XXX Corps, making for the village of Wyler in order to open up the Nijmegen–Cleve road.

OVERLEAF **By blowing dykes and opening dams, the Germans flooded the lower Rhine valley forming a seemingly impenetrable area of low-lying flood land on the border of Holland and Germany. This area linked with the formidable fixed defences of the Siegfried Line effectively blocked the northern route into Germany.**

3rd Canadian Division was given the task of securing the flooded area on the left flank of the main British/Canadian thrust – Operation Veritable. This entailed assaulting enemy-held isolated villages which appeared as islands in the flat waterlogged landscape. Dotted through the still waters were buildings and farms, some of which were fortified by the enemy into well-defended strong points.

Tony Bryan. 04/00

The road was reached without too much difficulty, but it took until 1830hrs in the evening before it was cleared. On their right were the 15th Scottish Division commanded by MajGen Barber, supported by 6th Guards Tank Brigade, with their axis of advance being along the road towards Cleve. As the troops came to grips with the enemy they found the defenders dazed and overwhelmed by the long bombardment. Opposition was at first slight, with the main delay caused by the minefields. Resistance stiffened, however, as the advance progressed.

Because of the narrowness of the front allocated to 15th Division, only a small part of its strength could be employed at first, but progress was maintained which allowed the right-hand of the division – the 46th Brigade – to take the village of Frasselt, overlooking Kranenburg, by early evening. The left-hand of the Scottish Division, the 227th Brigade, fared less well initially when the Germans manning the defences in front of them put up a stubborn resistance. The Argyll and Sutherland

Highlanders lost every officer in its forward company within minutes. Most of the supporting tanks were bogged down in the mud, but relentless pressure applied by the Scotsmen allowed progress to be made and the town of Kranenburg was occupied by 1700hrs. The main road between Kranenburg and Cleve was waterlogged to a depth of several feet and stoutly defended, so the advance temporarily switched inland. The division's new thrust employed its reserve brigade, the 44th, to break through the Siegfried defences and seize the heavily defended area around Nutterden and open the main road into Cleve. It was then intended for the remaining two brigades to attack Cleve itself. Once the town had fallen, the 43rd Wessex Division, commanded by MajGen Ivor Thomas, would pass through and exploit the open ground beyond, wheeling south towards Goch at the rear of the Reichswald, outflanking any German defenders holed up in the forest.

The 44th Brigade intended to attack the fortifications of the Westwall with their armoured breaching force, which consisted of Churchill tanks of the Grenadier Guards, flame-throwing Crocodile tanks and a battery of self-propelled guns. In the event, much of this armour was bogged down either in the mud or in the vast traffic jams that clogged the roads forward. Enough striking force did, however, get forward to join in the attack and Nutterden was reached in the early hours of the next morning after protracted fighting.

To the right of the 15th Division were the two units making the frontal assault on the Reichswald: the 53rd Welsh Division under the command of MajGen R. K. Ross and 51st Highland Division commanded by MajGen T. G. Rennie. These two divisions came out of the smoke at 1030hrs, following closely behind the rolling barrage, and plunged into the forest. The Welsh Division was on the left of this attack next to the Scottish Division and advanced with 71st Brigade up front across an open valley against little opposition. The brigade traversed the anti-tank ditch and swept into the north-west angle of the Reichswald, taking its objective, an area of high ground called the Brandenburg Height, at

33

RIGHT **Troops of 152nd Brigade move down one of the main rides through the southern half of the Reichswald, following behind a Churchill Crocodile flame-thrower from 34th Armoured Brigade. This ride was one of the main axes for the 51st Division and was code-named 'Oregon'. The brigade had been held up by a German counter-attack on 9 February and were now, on 10 February, advancing with the help of armour.** (Imperial War Museum)

1400hrs. Tank support had mostly bogged down in the thick mud during the advance, although some Churchill tanks had got through and kept up with the forward troops. 160th Brigade now took over the front and made it to the main part of the Siegfried defences around midnight.

The Welsh Division's neighbour to the south was the 51st Highland Division. It had the most difficult of all the fighting that day, having to clear a wide sector of the front from a narrow base. Major-General Rennie attacked with a reinforced 154th Brigade, but had the misfortune to meet the paratroopers of the 2nd Parachute Regiment (Lackner) that Schlemm had moved there just days before. The division did not reach the edge of the forest until night was falling. Here 152nd Brigade took over the advance and plunged through the breach and into the woods, spending the rest of the night clearing a path. 153rd Brigade now entered the fight and forced itself onto the high ground at the south-west corner of the Reichswald, although its start had been delayed by the traffic of 152nd Brigade moving forward.

The fighting on the first day of 'Veritable' had not reached all of the initial objectives, but XXX Corps had made a promising start. The Canadian 3rd Division, commanded by MajGen Dan Spry, now began its part in the offensive when it took to the water in Buffaloes and began clearing the fortified villages to the north of the 15th Division. The blown dykes on the Maas and Rhine had created vast inland waterways. These waterlogged areas were obviously a problem to the advance, but they did aid the Canadians in one sense: the depth of water covering the deadly minefields and tank traps allowed the Buffaloes, full of infantry, to sail over the worst of the fixed defences with impunity. Spry's 'water rats' chugged out into the darkness to make waterborne assaults on the marooned islands which were isolated from each other in the floodwater. Many of these villages were well defended and it was a particularly difficult and costly task for the Canadians to clear them of the enemy, but by first light the Canadian infantry had captured all of its objectives and continued with its sweep to clear the flooded flat lands.

All along the front fighting went on throughout the night. In some places the main defenders had fallen back into the prepared bunkers of

A knocked-out Valentine XI tank has succumbed to the rising waters along the Nijmegen–Cleve road just after the opening of 'Veritable'.
(Imperial War Museum)

the Westwall, while elsewhere, especially against the Highland Division, seasoned troops clung on tenaciously to every last piece of ground. When morning came, the advance continued. The Canadian 2nd Division had been 'pinched' out of the attack as the front narrowed around Kranenburg. The 15th Division, with flank protection supplied by the 'naval' forces of Canadian 3rd Division, resumed its advance towards Cleve. Although a few hours behind schedule, Gen Horrocks believed that it was time to call up the 43rd Division to exploit the capture of the town. He put it on one hour's notice to move from midday and signalled for the Scotsmen to 'press forward'.

The Canadian Army's attack had caused consternation in the German camp. Was this the start of the long-awaited offensive in the north or just a spoiling attack made to take attention away from the site of a bigger assault across the Maas in the south? Those commanders in the area – Fiebig, Straube and Schlemm – believed the former, while higher command were not convinced. Schlemm did, however, persuade his army group commander, Blaskowitz, to release the 7th Parachute Division, commanded by GenLt Wolfgang Erdmann, for the battle. Elements of this division were rushed forward to bolster the eastern defences of Cleve, especially the high ground to the west of Materborn.

The Materborn feature was also the objective of the 15th Scottish Division on the second day of the battle. The Scotsmen arrived on the western side of the feature just as the German 7th Parachute Division arrived on the eastern face. The two sides clashed with great force on a spur called the Bresserberg. A severe firefight took place throughout the day which resulted in the Scottish Division achieving control of the whole of the Materborn feature. Reconnaissance patrols found that Cleve seemed to be lightly held by dazed German troops and Horrocks received reports that the 15th Scottish were moving into the outskirts of the town. These optimistic reports convinced the corps commander that it was time to introduce the 43rd Wessex Division into the battle. This was a bad move.

At this point on the second day the whole front was suffering from the complete collapse of the roads in the rear. The main Nijmegen–Cleve road was flooded by the ever rising water from the

blown dykes and was difficult to negotiate, as it was impossible to move off the road due to the surrounding waterlogged ground. Other roads forward were either secondary roads that were lightly metalled and beginning to disintegrate, or sandy tracks which had been reduced to seas of glutinous mud. The heavy rain of the past few days showed little sign of stopping. Great traffic jams began to build up as tanks, troops and supplies tried to make their way forward. The battle was becoming a logistical nightmare. It was into this chaos that 43rd Division now attempted to get forward to exploit the breakthrough. The axis of the 43rd's advance, the Nijmegen–Cleve road, was already in use by the forward units of the 15th Division, who were trying to fight a difficult battle. The arrival of the Wessexmen and their transport led to a foul-up of monumental proportions.

Elsewhere on the battlefield slow progress was being made. The Welsh Division had pushed on with 160th Brigade to take two more features in the Reichswald – the Geldenburg and the Stoppelburg – cutting the minor road which passed through the forest from Kranenburg to Hekkens, and had reached the northern edge of the Reichswald alongside 15th Division with the 158th Brigade. The Highland Division continued its advance within the forest with 152nd Brigade, brushed aside a German counter-attack, and had reached the Kranenburg–Hekkens road. Outside, to the south of the Reichswald, 153rd Brigade moved over open country towards Gennep alongside the River Maas. Thus by the end of the second day, most of the original objectives had been taken. With the Americans due to launch 'Grenade' the next day, 10 February, Horrocks could afford to take some risks to keep the operation on schedule, for the attack across the Roer in the south would at least stop German reinforcements being moved north against him and might well attract some German units away from him.

Before Operation Grenade could start, however, there was the matter of the Roer dams to consider. Simpson had his 9th Army lined up against the River Roer ready to attack across it and link up with Montgomery, but he could not risk committing his troops over the river with the dams still intact or uncaptured. It was clear that should he do so, the Germans would blow the seven dams and release the 3,920 cubic feet

(111 million cubic metres) of water to create a vast floodland which
would isolate his forces over the river for days or even weeks. The dams
had to be captured.

The problem of the Roer dams had been appreciated since the
previous November when 9th Army arrived on the river, but they were
located in 1st Army's zone. It was difficult to get anyone to take their
capture seriously enough to make it a high priority. Attempts by the RAF
were made to bomb the dams, but other than superficial damage to the
Erft dam, the raids were not successful. In early December Hodges gave
the problem over to Gen Gerow's US V Corps. On 13 December Gerow's
troops attacked towards the dams. The assault did not lack strength,
consisting as it did of three divisions – 8th, 78th and 99th Infantry
Divisions – plus the 102nd Cavalry Group and a combat command from
5th Armored Division, but the whole scheme lacked impetus and failed
to get anywhere near the objectives.

The seven dams were located in the heart of the Westwall, with two
belts of fortifications guarding the large backwaters behind them. The
whole area was a network of steep-sided gorges and small mountains,
covered in pine trees and deep with snow. The roads were narrow and
winding, with virtually each bend covered by an enemy pillbox. Progress
along the mountainsides was extremely slow and hazardous. The
three-pronged attack on the dams immediately ran into trouble as it
battered the bunkers of the first belt of the Siegfried Line. After three days
of fighting, and with the loss of 2,500 men (half of whom were non-battle
casualties), the penetration achieved no more than 2 miles (3.2km). On
the fourth day of the operation things ground to a complete halt. The
attack had the misfortune to run headlong into the opening moves of
Hitler's great Ardennes offensive. The 'Battle of the Bulge' had started.

It took until the end of January 1945 for US 1st Army to push the
enemy back to the line they held at the start of their offensive. Only then
could the problem of the Roer dams be once again considered. By that
time planning for the 'Veritable'/'Grenade' attack was well in hand. It
was clear to everyone now that the dams had to be captured before the
great push in the north could be undertaken. Preliminary moves to
achieve this were made on 30 January. On 2 February, Gen Heubner

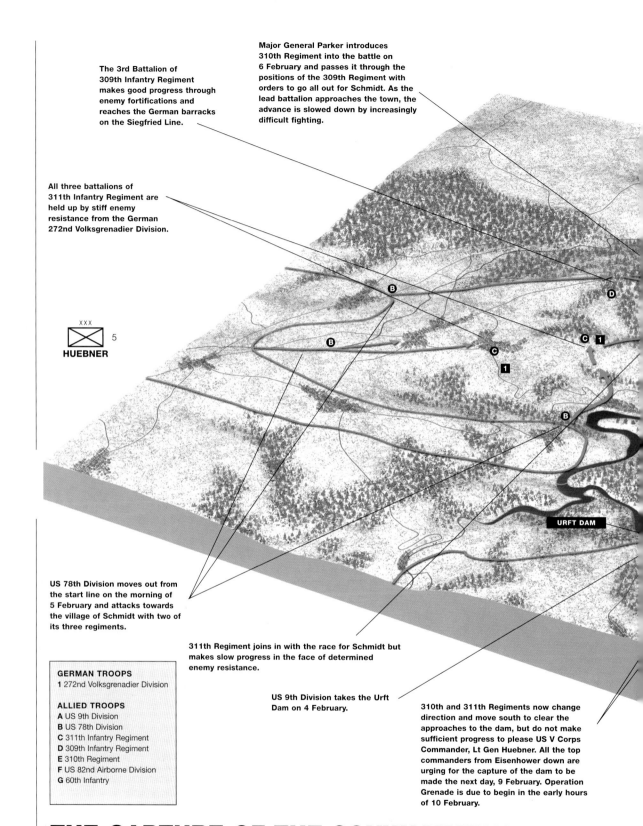

The 3rd Battalion of
309th Infantry Regiment
makes good progress through
enemy fortifications and
reaches the German barracks
on the Siegfried Line.

Major General Parker introduces
310th Regiment into the battle on
6 February and passes it through the
positions of the 309th Regiment with
orders to go all out for Schmidt. As the
lead battalion approaches the town, the
advance is slowed down by increasingly
difficult fighting.

All three battalions of
311th Infantry Regiment are
held up by stiff enemy
resistance from the German
272nd Volksgrenadier Division.

XXX
5
HUEBNER

B

D

B

C

C

1

1

B

URFT DAM

US 78th Division moves out from
the start line on the morning of
5 February and attacks towards
the village of Schmidt with two of
its three regiments.

311th Regiment joins in with the race for Schmidt but
makes slow progress in the face of determined
enemy resistance.

GERMAN TROOPS
1 272nd Volksgrenadier Division

ALLIED TROOPS
A US 9th Division
B US 78th Division
C 311th Infantry Regiment
D 309th Infantry Regiment
E 310th Regiment
F US 82nd Airborne Division
G 60th Infantry

US 9th Division takes the Urft
Dam on 4 February.

310th and 311th Regiments now change
direction and move south to clear the
approaches to the dam, but do not make
sufficient progress to please US V Corps
Commander, Lt Gen Huebner. All the top
commanders from Eisenhower down are
urging for the capture of the dam to be
made the next day, 9 February. Operation
Grenade is due to begin in the early hours
of 10 February.

THE CAPTURE OF THE SCHWAMMENAUEL DAM
5 – 9 FEBRUARY 1945

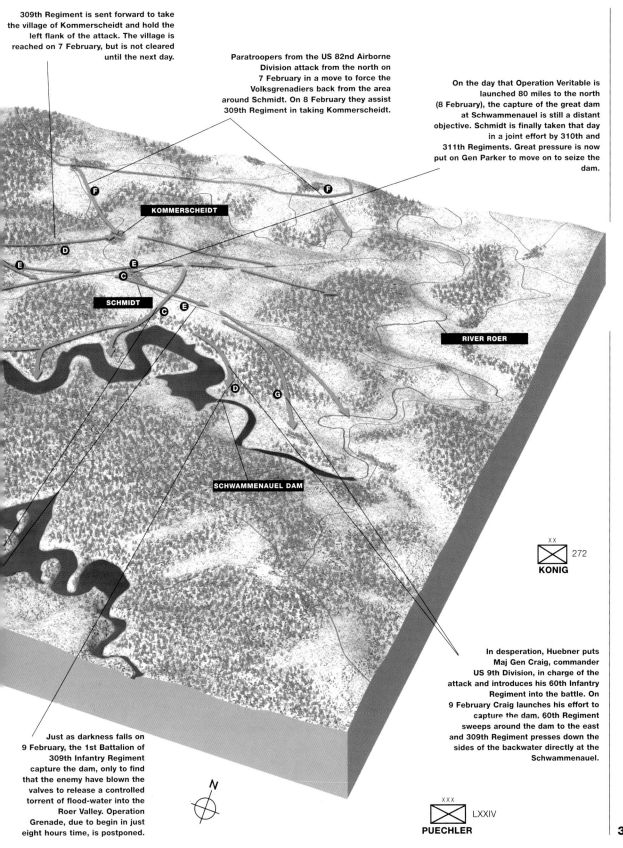

309th Regiment is sent forward to take the village of Kommerscheidt and hold the left flank of the attack. The village is reached on 7 February, but is not cleared until the next day.

Paratroopers from the US 82nd Airborne Division attack from the north on 7 February in a move to force the Volksgrenadiers back from the area around Schmidt. On 8 February they assist 309th Regiment in taking Kommerscheidt.

On the day that Operation Veritable is launched 80 miles to the north (8 February), the capture of the great dam at Schwammenauel is still a distant objective. Schmidt is finally taken that day in a joint effort by 310th and 311th Regiments. Great pressure is now put on Gen Parker to move on to seize the dam.

F

F

KOMMERSCHEIDT

D

E

E

C

SCHMIDT

C

E

RIVER ROER

D

G

SCHWAMMENAUEL DAM

xx
272
KONIG

In desperation, Huebner puts Maj Gen Craig, commander US 9th Division, in charge of the attack and introduces his 60th Infantry Regiment into the battle. On 9 February Craig launches his effort to capture the dam, 60th Regiment sweeps around the dam to the east and 309th Regiment presses down the sides of the backwater directly at the Schwammenauel.

Just as darkness falls on 9 February, the 1st Battalion of 309th Infantry Regiment capture the dam, only to find that the enemy have blown the valves to release a controlled torrent of flood-water into the Roer Valley. Operation Grenade, due to begin in just eight hours time, is postponed.

N

xxx
LXXIV
PUECHLER

(who had taken over command of US V Corps from Gen Gerow) gave MajGen Edwin Parker orders for his 78th Infantry Division to capture the village of Schmidt together with the largest and most important of all the dams, the Schwammenauel. Parker was told that the operation was the most vital at that time on the entire Western Front, as indeed it was.

The task was a tall order for the 78th Division who had only limited battle experience. Parker's division set out through the close country at 0300hrs on 5 February, just five days before the scheduled start of 'Grenade'. The next day the adjacent division, the 9th Infantry, had managed to capture the Erft dam intact and hopes were high for a successful operation. The 78th Division slipped through the outer pillboxes of the Westwall with little difficulty, then things went bad. The closely wooded country and the lack of any supporting fire made progress extremely slow. In an effort to achieve the breakthrough, Parker put all three of his regiments into the attack, urged on personally by his corps and army commanders. Armour tried to get up with the leading troops but the enemy covered all the routes.

Inexorably, time slipped by and the pressure for success rose. By 8 February – the day that 'Veritable' was launched – the 78th Division had still not taken Schmidt, the village overlooking the Schwammenauel dam. Shortly before noon, Hodges telephoned Heubner and expressed his dissatisfaction: Bradley, Simpson, Montgomery, Crerar and Horrocks were all waiting for news. Heubner piled on the pressure. He shifted a regimental combat team from 9th Division, together with the 9th's divisional commander, MajGen Louis Craig, across to Schmidt and told Craig to take over 78th Division's men and seize the Schwammenauel.

Despite the introduction of a new commander and a veteran unit, the going was slow again on 9 February. It was not until darkness had fallen that the leading regiment, 309th Infantry, approached the Schwammenauel. Sending two groups of the 1st Battalion onto the dam, one to cross over the top and one to move against the lower level, the structure was captured. Engineers searched for demolitions, expecting the Germans to blow the dam at any moment: small arms fire picked off the troops as they scrambled over buildings. Just after midnight, in the early hours of 10 February, they finally penetrated the lower tunnels and began looking for explosives. They found none. Enemy troops had done all the damage they intended to do: they had blown the machinery and destroyed the discharge valves. The damage did not cause a major cascade of water, but a steady and powerful flow that would create a long lasting flood all the way down the River Roer. The Schwammenauel's reservoir would take weeks to empty. Operation Grenade could no longer go ahead that day and was postponed.

Seventy miles (112.7km) to the north, 'Veritable' staggered on. Montgomery knew that with the Americans unable to launch their attack, the Germans would move troops up to the North to counter his attack now that it was safe for Von Rundstedt to do so. It was a setback which would cost the Canadians and British dearly, but in the final analysis, Monty was not too displeased. He was the overall commander for both operations and as long as Crerar could hold the enemy in the north, hammering away at him in a battle of blind attrition, the American operation, when it was launched, would be against much lighter opposition than first envisaged. As Montgomery said at the time: 'When Grenade is finally launched it should produce quicker results'. To bolster the forces available to Crerar, Montgomery gained two American divisions from Eisenhower to take over the line held by British 2nd Army's 52nd Lowland and 11th Armoured Divisions, and release the two units for the Rhineland operation.

So Horrocks pressed on into the Reichswald. On 10 February, the third day of the battle, the Welsh and Highland Divisions pushed on through and alongside the Reichswald. In the north of the battlefield, the 15th Scottish nibbled away at Cleve while the Canadian 3rd Division continued to hold the northern flank as waterborne infantry. The 43rd Wessex Division crawled its way through the traffic jam that had clogged all the routes forward and its leading brigade, 129th Brigade, tried to slip round the south of Cleve. In the darkness, it took a wrong turn, ended up in the town itself and was forced to fight a vicious battle, much to the surprise of the German defenders–and the 15th Scottish Division who were planning their own assault on the town. The Wessexmen were immediately embroiled in difficult street fighting, for the whole town was a smouldering ruin. The air-raids sanctioned by Horrocks at the start of the battle had flattened Cleve. All streets were choked with rubble; fallen buildings blocked every pathway and enormous craters provided perfect positions for the enemy defenders. There was no clear way through Cleve along the blocked highways, the route eastwards was completely closed. Horrocks' bombing of the city had backfired on him.

The capture of Cleve was one of the first and most important of the initial objectives assigned to 'Veritable'. Horrocks had hoped to have the town in his possession on the first day and to be able to exploit its possession in order to wheel southwards and take Goch. Enemy resistance all around the town was making this impossible. On this third day of the battle, new German units were coming into the line to bottle up the Canadian 1st Army in and around the Reichswald. One of the first to arrive was the German 6th Parachute Division commanded by GenLt Hermann Plocher. Advance elements of this division barred the way to the 53rd Welsh Division in the middle of the forest. The remainder of XLVII Corps (Von Luttwitz), the Wehrmacht's mobile reserve, was also committed to the battle. Seasoned panzer troops now began to replace the wrecked remnants of the German 84th Division who had taken the full force of the Allied attack. Resistance began to stiffen considerably.

The next few days saw a stand-up slogging match between the two opposing forces. For XXX Corps there were no quick gains to be had, just a few yards of waterlogged ground taken at a high price. To the men of both sides the battlefield resembled the worst days of World War I. They lived and fought in trenches and pillboxes, suffered tremendous artillery bombardments and struggled to keep dry in the appalling conditions. The rain was incessant. Supplies were difficult to get forward over roads that had collapsed under the pounding of the traffic. Everywhere the cloying mud bogged down the tanks, whilst flame and shot shattered the unwary. And all the while the pressure to get forward, to make progress and to move on did not let up.

Cleve was finally taken and cleared on the 11th by the Scottish Division together with the Canadian 3rd Division who had landed from their Buffaloes and advanced down the west bank of the Spoy Canal into the

Tony Bryan. 04/00

During the mid-afternoon of 11 February under an overcast sky, the 53rd Welsh Division made their attack on this German machine-gun post in the Reichswald Forest. It was the third day of the battle and the German defenders were falling back and moving rapidly to new defensive positions as they were forced to give up their previous ones. The defenders had therefore been in action continuously for three days and were becoming tired, depleted and disorganised.

The new defensive positions included improvised bunkers built of wood and sand bags, covered in earth; few of these such bunkers showed any signs of long occupancy. They were mostly equipped with weapons removed from bunkers on the western side of the forest just before they were overrun. German tactics were to delay the enemy for as long as possible and then retire to the next defensive position.

town. The presence of the 43rd Division to the south of the town was also having the desired effect; German forces were unable to stabilise the line and block the Wessex Division's steady progress around to the east. Fighting was hard, but little by little the Wessexmen gained the upper hand, although their long tail of vehicles, guns and supporting arms only added to the immobilised mass of troops and armour along the flooded road back to Kranenburg. Both the 43rd and 15th Divisions struggled with, and often against, each other to get their formations into a fighting position.

For XXX Corps, the next few days were spent slowly consolidating the ground taken by force, and applying relentless pressure to a stubborn enemy. The 53rd Division crossed the Cleve–Gennep road in the heart of the Reichswald, heading for both the eastern edge of the woods and the southern fringe that opened out onto the River Niers. The 51st Division attacked the important crossroads at Hekkens in the south of the forest, took the little hamlet and headed west for Gennep to clear the open land between the Reichswald and the Maas. The 43rd Division took the villages of Materborn, Hau and Bedburg and established itself clear of the suburbs of Cleve, facing south towards Goch. In the meantime, Von Luttwitz moved his two panzer divisions from XLVII Corps up to counter-attack and retake Cleve. The 15th Panzer Grenadier Division, commanded by GenMaj Wolfgang Maucke, positioned itself south of Cleve between the square Forest of Cleve and the Reichswald and sent a battle group into the woods towards the advancing Welshmen in an attempt to get to Cleve from the south. The clash was spirited and costly; the Welsh battalions held their ground with small arms and mortars while the divisional artillery pounded the attackers. The deluge of high explosives broke up the move and put the 15th Panzer Grenadiers to flight.

Generalmajor Siegfried von Waldenburg advanced with his 116th Panzer Division westwards to Bedburg, the village that had been just recently taken by the British 43rd Division. On 12 February Von Waldenburg hit the 43rd Division, but the attack, although heavy, lacked sufficient strength to break the Wessexmen. Overwhelming artillery fire decimated the Germans and broke up their advance. The German corps commander realised that Cleve could not be retaken and so Von Luttwitz went on the defensive. Schlemm ordered that XLVII Corps should hold a line extending from Hasselt on the Calcar road, along the Eselberg ridge just south of Bedburg to the edge of the north-west corner of the Forest of Cleve. Von Luttwitz deployed his divisions with the remnants of 84th Division on the right, the 15th Panzer Grenadiers on the left and elements of 116th Panzers supporting both of them. The German 346th Division, commanded by

Troops from the Highland Light Infantry of the 15th Scottish Division roll a large wooden swastika along the streets of Kranenburg just after its capture. The men intend to use the trophy as firewood. In the background, a British tank crewman dressed in an oversuit looks on.
(Imperial War Museum)

GenMaj Walter Steinmueller, newly arrived in the area, also joined the battle.

Now began the advance that turned 'Veritable'. Major-General Thomas was given orders to attack south with his 43rd Wessex Division and take Goch. The advance began on 13 February when the 5th Wiltshires, of 129th Brigade, pressed forward to the high ground south-east of Bedburg to secure a start line for their sister battalion, the 4th. This second battalion was ordered to capture the hamlet of Trippenburg and a vital set of crossroads. A heavy counter-barrage laid down by the enemy caught the 5th Wiltshires as they deployed and set off for the ridge, but they pressed on grimly and took the low heights. The 4th Wiltshires now passed through with the main attack. In driving rain the troops moved out across the slopes supported by the Shermans of 8th Armoured Brigade's Nottinghamshire Yeomanry. The heavy tanks with their narrow tracks soon found the thick mud impassable and most were bogged down. The Wiltshiremen struggled on in the face of withering fire from the German defenders. Devoid of armoured protection, the exposed infantry doggedly prodded home their attack. Trippenburg was reached as darkness fell and cleared by midnight. It had taken all day, but the outer crust of the Von Luttwitz defensive line had been pierced. During the night the 4th Wiltshires repulsed a counter-attack by paratroopers backed by Tiger and Mark IV tanks during which a complete company was overrun. In the morning 5th Wiltshires came forward and continued the attack. They struggled throughout the hours of daylight to cover just a few hundred yards to the vital crossroads. In front of them, the 15th Panzer Grenadiers made them pay dearly for every foot of ground taken. All senior officers of the battalion bar one were casualties. Shell-fire continued unabated. Night came and still the Wiltshires fought on, straining their way forward in the dark. Eventually their superhuman effort won the day and they took the crossroads, 400 yards (364m) east of the Forest of Cleve. They had suffered over 200 casualties.

Thomas now committed 130th Brigade into the battle. The lead battalion, 4th Dorsets, formed up under fire and set out for Goch. It was

A Churchill tank from 147th Hampshire Regiment RAC makes a path through the Reichswald on 10 February. The forest was thought to be impenetrable to armour, but tank crews found a way through the forest by deducing that if the trees were small enough and close together they could be pushed over and if they were too large for this, then they were wide enough apart to pass between. The use of armour in the middle of such a densely wooded area came as a shock to the Germans.
(Imperial War Museum)

the same as the previous two days: infantry pressing forward through ferocious defensive fire and tenaciously resisting countless enemy counter-attacks. A fresh new German formation, Battle Group Hutze, now loomed up before the Wessexmen. The infantry battle continued with machine gun, shell and mortar fire criss-crossing the area. As the Dorsets tired, the 7th Hampshires took over the advance. The fighting continued with equal ferocity. Day passed again into night, still the struggle went on, each side pounding the other in a slugging match that would eventually see one or the other collapse. Now the 5th Dorsets came forward and took up the gauntlet. As they struck out for their objective, counter-attacks came from the rear and hit the Hampshires, while withering fire from the enemy in the Forest of Cleve raked the 5th Dorsets' right flank.

Major-General Thomas had decided that all troops engaged on both sides were nearing the limit of their endurance. It was time for a bold stroke. He ordered 130th Brigade to push on its attack with all three battalions and capture a new start line 800 yards (728m) south-east of the Forest of Cleve. He now intended to launch the fresh 214th Brigade on a two-battalion front straight down the road to Goch. It was a masterful move timed to perfection. When, at 1520hrs on 16 February, the two lead battalions of 214 Brigade – 7th Somerset Light Infantry and 1st Worcestershires – arrived at the start line, 130th Brigade had only just captured it. They did not pause; the divisional artillery immediately opened up with a rolling barrage and the two new lead battalions surged out into the flat open countryside. The momentum of the attack, even though some of the armour was initially left behind, took the enemy by surprise. There was no let-up, most sections had the support of a tank from the 4th/7th Dragoon Guards which blasted every building and strong point they came across. Those whose tanks had not yet reached them pressed on regardless. Every German that resisted was shot dead. In the first two hours the 7th Somersets had advanced over 2,000 yards (1,820m), by nightfall they had covered 3,000 yards (2,730m). Alongside them, the 1st Worcestershires kept pace.

BRITISH 43RD (WESSEX) DIVISION ADVANCE TO THE GOCH ESCARPMENT, 13 – 17 FEBRUARY 1945

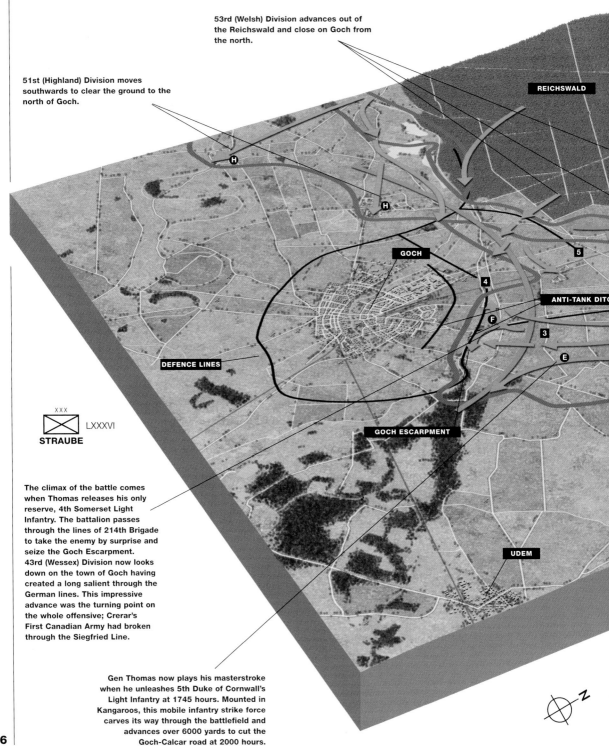

53rd (Welsh) Division advances out of the Reichswald and close on Goch from the north.

51st (Highland) Division moves southwards to clear the ground to the north of Goch.

REICHSWALD

GOCH

5

4

ANTI-TANK DITC

F

3

E

DEFENCE LINES

XXX

LXXXVI

STRAUBE

GOCH ESCARPMENT

The climax of the battle comes when Thomas releases his only reserve, 4th Somerset Light Infantry. The battalion passes through the lines of 214th Brigade to take the enemy by surprise and seize the Goch Escarpment. 43rd (Wessex) Division now looks down on the town of Goch having created a long salient through the German lines. This impressive advance was the turning point on the whole offensive; Crerar's First Canadian Army had broken through the Siegfried Line.

UDEM

Gen Thomas now plays his masterstroke when he unleashes 5th Duke of Cornwall's Light Infantry at 1745 hours. Mounted in Kangaroos, this mobile infantry strike force carves its way through the battlefield and advances over 6000 yards to cut the Goch-Calcar road at 2000 hours.

N

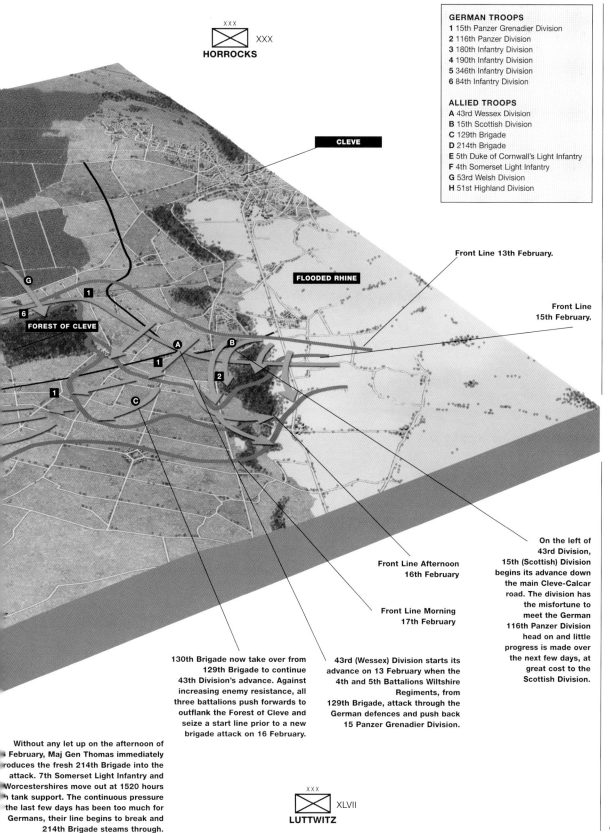

HORROCKS XXX

GERMAN TROOPS
1 15th Panzer Grenadier Division
2 116th Panzer Division
3 180th Infantry Division
4 190th Infantry Division
5 346th Infantry Division
6 84th Infantry Division

ALLIED TROOPS
A 43rd Wessex Division
B 15th Scottish Division
C 129th Brigade
D 214th Brigade
E 5th Duke of Cornwall's Light Infantry
F 4th Somerset Light Infantry
G 53rd Welsh Division
H 51st Highland Division

CLEVE

FLOODED RHINE

FOREST OF CLEVE

Front Line 13th February.

Front Line
15th February.

Front Line Afternoon
16th February

Front Line Morning
17th February

On the left of
43rd Division,
15th (Scottish) Division
begins its advance down
the main Cleve-Calcar
road. The division has
the misfortune to
meet the German
116th Panzer Division
head on and little
progress is made over
the next few days, at
great cost to the
Scottish Division.

130th Brigade now take over from
129th Brigade to continue
43rd Division's advance. Against
increasing enemy resistance, all
three battalions push forwards to
outflank the Forest of Cleve and
seize a start line prior to a new
brigade attack on 16 February.

43rd (Wessex) Division starts its
advance on 13 February when the
4th and 5th Battalions Wiltshire
Regiments, from
129th Brigade, attack through the
German defences and push back
15 Panzer Grenadier Division.

Without any let up on the afternoon of
February, Maj Gen Thomas immediately
roduces the fresh 214th Brigade into the
attack. 7th Somerset Light Infantry and
Worcestershires move out at 1520 hours
h tank support. The continuous pressure
the last few days has been too much for
Germans, their line begins to break and
214th Brigade steams through.

XXX
LUTTWITZ XLVII

A signals line party working along the Nijmegen–Cleve road near Kranenburg. The Germans had blown dykes on the River Rhine and the water levels rose steadily throughout the first few days of 'Veritable'. This main road became impassable to wheeled vehicles and all movement had to be switched to the roads closer to the Reichswald. The signallers are moving forward in amphibious Weasels and DUKWs. (Imperial War Museum)

Now Thomas played his masterstroke. The 5th Duke of Cornwall Light Infantry, its men mounted in Kangaroos (turretless tanks) and supported by B squadron of the 4th/7th Dragoon Guards, arrived at the village of Blacknik. They then deployed into five columns and headed due south, hell-bent for the villages of Imigshof, Bergmanshoff and Schroenshof, 6,000 yards (5,460m) ahead. In the words of the Brigade Commander, Brigadier Hubert Essame: 'This overwhelming stroke was too much for the enemy. In the dark and confusion, he went to ground.' The DCLI made it to the villages, turned out the defenders and cut the important road from Goch to Calcar, splitting the enemy defences in half. The 43rd Division's only reserve, the 4th Somerset Light Infantry, was now set loose to complete Thomas' plan. In a night attack, they surprised the enemy by slipping through the advance battalions and made for the escarpment overlooking Goch. Catching the German defenders completely by surprise, they seized the escarpment and had consolidated their possession of it by dawn. The 43rd Division now held the commanding ground looking down on Goch, just 1,000 yards (910m) away. It was the turning point in the battle.

The spectacular success of the Wessex Division in carving out a great salient in the German line, caused much consternation to the enemy and split his defences wide open, but he was stubbornly resisting everywhere else he was in contact with the Canadian 1st Army. In the Reichswald the Welsh Division had made it through the forest and broke out into the open overlooking the flank of the 43rd Division. Horrocks now ordered the division to close up with the 43rd and take the escarpment from east of the railway that led from Cleve to Goch. The 51st Highland Division, reinforced with the 32nd Guards Brigade from the Guards Armoured Division, had made steady progress along the ground between the Maas and the Reichswald, crossing the small River Niers and taking Kessel. It now pressed on up the Niers towards Goch. On the extreme right of the Highlanders, the 52nd Lowland Division had been introduced to the battle on 14 February, with instructions to advance alongside the Maas

Infantry from the 2nd Seaforth Highlanders of the British 51st Division advance through the Reichswald. In the background a Churchill Crocodile flame-thrower tank rumbles forward ready to deal with a strong point that the battalion had encountered during the advance. (Imperial War Museum)

from Gennep and take the villages of Afferden and Well and then swing behind Goch towards the east. Four divisions were now pressing Goch and its defence line: the heavily fortified town had now become the western cornerstone of the German defences. The German garrison in Goch included 180th and 190th Infantry Divisions together with the 2nd Parachute Regiment, all part of Gen Straube's LXXXVI Corps.

As the 43rd Division were approaching Goch, the 15th Scottish were pushing forward along the road from Cleve to Calcar. They ran into the 116th Panzer Division and suffered a bloody rebuff. The advance started on 12 February but two days of fighting saw 15th Division halted around the Moyland Woods. On the 14th some changes to the command structure were made by Gen Crerar. The fighting had moved past the narrow confines of the corridor between the Rhine and the Maas and the front was now opening up across the rolling land behind the Reichswald. Crerar now introduced the Canadian II Corps, under the command of LtGen Simonds, as a component force. Comprising the 15th Scottish Division and the Canadian 2nd and 3rd Divisions, Canadian II Corps took over the responsibility for the left wing of Canadian 1st Army. The Canadian 4th Armored Division and the British 11th Armoured Division were held in reserve to exploit any breakthrough.

Simonds withdrew the 15th Scottish from the Calcar road and replaced it with the two Canadian infantry divisions. The 3rd Division tried again for the Moyland Woods and spent several days attempting to take command of the Cleve–Calcar road. The 2nd Division meanwhile put in a set-piece attack on 19 February, striking south-east from Louisendorf to cross the Calcar–Goch road. Two battalions of the division crossed the road and consolidated for the night. Around midnight, they were counter-attacked by Battle Group Hauser, a combat team from the crack Panzer Lehr Division who had been refitting nearby in Marienbaum. Together with the 116th Panzer Division, Battle Group Hauser caught the Canadians just after they had sent their armour back for refuelling and rearming. The two battalions were all but wiped out and survivors were sent reeling. Through the night and into the next day the battle raged and the Germans gradually forced the Canadians back. In the late morning Sherman tanks from the Glengarry Horse and the Queen's Own Cameron Highlanders arrived and restored the balance. Then 17-pdr (7.65kg) anti-tank guns moved into position and attacked the exposed Jagdpanthers and the Germans began to falter. By the end of the afternoon, the Panzer divisions had started to pull back. The

An infantryman takes cover during the bombardment of Goch. The attack by 51st Highland Division from the south of Goch caught the German garrison by surprise. The German commandant, Colonel Mutussek, had moved the bulk of his troops over the River Niers within the town to counter the attack from the north by 15th Scottish Division. (Imperial War Museum)

German counter-attack had fizzled out through lack of strength, but the Canadians' advance had also been forced to halt. There was now a pause in the battle while Crerar worked out what the next moves might be.

Whilst the Canadians had been pressing towards Calcar, XXX Corps were poised to take Goch. The 43rd Division ensconced on the escarpment overlooking the town began bridging the anti-tank ditch at the base of the feature and on 8 February sent the 7th Somerset Light Infantry down into the outskirts of the town. The battalion actually got across a second anti-tank ditch in the suburbs and deployed within the town itself, regardless of their own division's artillery fire. But this attack was a diversion for the big event, for the two Scottish divisions, the 15th and the 51st, were assigned to the capture of the town. The next day, the 51st put in a two-brigade attack from west of the River Niers using the 152nd and 153rd, as the 15th Division, recently returned to XXX Corps from the Canadians, used its 44th Brigade to open the attack east of the Niers. Both attacks carried with them a great mechanised train of armoured support in the shape of tanks, bridge-carriers, Kangaroos, bulldozers, flame-throwers and guns. The artillery barrage that shot them forward was tremendous. The opening moves were slow against the concrete defences and dug-in emplacements, with the 15th Scottish meeting especially spirited resistance from the German defenders. The garrison commander, Col Mutussek, had moved the bulk of his forces over the River Niers which ran through the town to counter the 15th Division, leaving the south more open for the 51st Highlanders. Too late he realised his mistake and the Highlanders poured into the town and over the bridge onto the eastern side. Close house-to-house fighting raged on throughout that day and into the next, but the Scottish divisions were in the town and were not going to be evicted. The Germans were caught unprepared for events and eventually succumbed to the all-round pressure. By the 22nd, Goch had fallen and been completely cleared of the enemy. Operation Veritable, the plan to break through the Westwall was over, but the battle was not yet won. All of Montgomery's troops now looked to the Rhine and the bridges at Wesel.

OPERATION GRENADE

By 21 February the flooded waters of the River Roer had started to recede. Lieutenant-General Bill Simpson, US 9th Army's commander, had been watching the level carefully for the past 11 days. His engineers had calculated that it would be at its lowest on about 25 February, but Bill Simpson wanted to take the Germans by surprise and so planned to launch his army across the Roer just before that date. He decided that the river level early on the morning of 23 February would be just low enough to make a crossing and, more importantly, bridging operations, possible. The attack would still be risky, for the fast-flowing water would be very lively, but the element of surprise would make it worth the risk.

Simpson's 9th Army was lined up along the River Roer on a front of 30 miles (48.3km), from north of Dueren to the confluence of the Maas and the Roer. The northern corps would head east across the Roer and then swing northwards to link up with Canadian 1st Army before turning eastwards again for the Rhine. The others would head north-east and

Men of the 309th Combat Engineers from the US 84th Division drag an assault boat to the banks of the River Roer at Linnich, prior to the assault in the early hours of 23 February. The steel boats were powered by paddle and carried one section of men. They were ungainly craft, square ended and very difficult to manoeuvre.
(National Archives, Washington)

Follow-up infantry of
US 29th Division from XIX Corps,
preparing to be called forward to
cross the River Roer on the first
day of Operation Grenade.
(National Archives, Washington)

east to close on the Rhine and clear the Rhineland. To protect his southern flank as his forces moved inland from the Roer, VII Corps from US 1st Army, commanded by MajGen J. Lawton Collins, would cross the Roer with its 104th Division (Allen) and 8th Division (Weaver) and advance alongside Simpson's extreme right-hand division.

Simpson had three corps with which to launch the assault. In the south, next to 1st Army's VII Corps, was Simpson's XIX Corps, commanded by MajGen Raymond McLain. On the right of XIX Corps' front was 29th Division (Gerhardt) with 30th Division (Hobbs) holding the river opposite Jülich. These two assaulting divisions had the back-up of 83rd Division (Macon) and 2nd Armored Division (White) behind them to exploit the breakout. The next corps to the north was MajGen Alvan Gillem's XIII Corps. Gillem intended to cross the river with his 102nd Division (Keating) on the right and 84th Division (Bolling) on the left at Linnich. In reserve he had the 5th Armored Division (Oliver). To the north was XVI Corps, commanded by MajGen John Anderson, a new formation as yet untried in battle. Anderson's corps was not to make an assault crossing, but to drive north along the west bank of the Roer and make an unopposed crossing when XIII Corps had cleared the area opposite. XVI Corps was then to take Roermond and drive north to link up with the Canadian 1st Army. The corps consisted of 35th Division (Baade), 79th Division (Wyche) and 8th Armored Division (Devine).

Operation Grenade began early on 23 February when, at 0245hrs, a tremendous artillery barrage lit up the dark skies. The guns of US

1st and 9th Armies, together with those of the British 2nd Army, laid down a massive bombardment on known and suspected German strong points across the River Roer. Over 1,500 guns hammered out all along the front for 45 intensive minutes. Then, as the barrage died away, the infantry of six divisions dragged their assault boats across muddy foreshores and into the river.

The most northerly of all the assault divisions was the 84th Division. It attacked from the centre of Linnich across a relatively narrow section of the river below the smashed road bridge at 0330hrs. The leading troops of the 1st Battalion, 334th Regiment, paddled their way over in 15-man assault craft through the swollen and violent river. The current was swift and merciless, sweeping aside any boat that had the misfortune to catch it broadside on. The first waves made it across with few casualties, but successive waves caught the force of the German defenders as they came up out of their shelters at the end of the artillery barrage. German small arms and mortar fire peppered the tiny craft as they made for the far side, but still the casualties were relatively light.

The orderly initial assault was followed by complete chaos. Many of the first waves of craft were still stuck on the far shore or had drifted downstream. When it came time for the next battalion, the 3rd Battalion, to cross, the footbridges the troops were supposed to have used were all out of action. One was not able to anchor on the far bank because of enemy fire, one was knocked out by a direct hit and the other was demolished by assault boats drifting down the river from the crossing site of the 102nd Division upstream of Linnich. As a result of these delays with the bridges, the 3rd Battalion was not able to start across the Roer

Infantry of the US 84th Division cross the River Roer dry shod on a footbridge at Linnich. The picture was taken on the first day of Operation Grenade. The bridge comprises a wooden treadway anchored to the storm boats used in the assault. (National Archives, Washington)

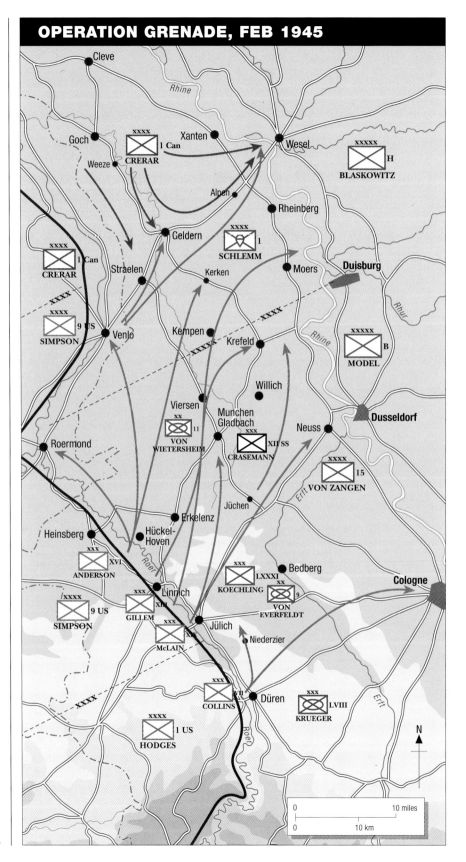

OPERATION GRENADE, FEB 1945

Cleve

Rhine

Goch

XXXX 1 Can
CRERAR

Weeze

Xanten

Wesel

XXXXX H
BLASKOWITZ

Alpen

Rheinberg

Geldern

XXXX 1
SCHLEMM

XXXX 1 Can
CRERAR

Straelen

Kerken

Moers

Duisburg

XXXX

Rhur

XXXX 9 US
SIMPSON

Venlo

Kempen

Krefeld

Rhine

XXXXX B
MODEL

XXXXX

Willich

Roermond

Viersen

Munchen
Gladbach

Neuss

Dusseldorf

xx 11
VON
WIETERSHEIM

xxx XII SS
CRASEMANN

XXXX 15
VON ZANGEN

Erft

Jüchen

Erkelenz

Heinsberg

Hückel-
Hoven

Roer

Bedberg

Cologne

xxx XVI
ANDERSON

Linnich

xxx LXXXI
KOECHLING

XXXXX 9 US
SIMPSON

xxx XIII
GILLEM

Jülich

xx 9
VON
EVERFELDT

xxx XIX
McLAIN

Niederzier

xxx VII
COLLINS

Düren

xxx LVIII
KRUEGER

Erft

XXXX

XXXX 1 US
HODGES

Roer

N

0 _____ 10 miles
0 _____ 10 km

TOP **The road bridge at Linnich, knocked out by artillery fire and bombing. The US 84th Division crossed the Roer just downstream to the right of the picture. (National Archives, Washington)**

RIGHT **Storm boats, used in the crossing of the Roer, have drifted from the crossing sites and have become caught on a blown bridge downstream. Many of the boats from the first waves of the assault were lost like these, forcing the subsequent waves to delay their crossings. This picture was taken in the XIX Corps' sector. (National Archives, Washington)**

until 0645hrs. All was not lost, however, for the 1st Battalion had seized the initiative. The men over the river had not stopped to clear the enemy from the far side, but had wheeled to the left and immediately moved downstream towards the village of Korrenzig. They pressed on regardless, taking the enemy by surprise, and were able to cover 2,000 yards (1,820m) and get into Korrenzig by 0610hrs, well before the follow-up battalion had even started to cross!

The 3rd Battalion completed its crossing using a shuttle service of boats at about 1035hrs. German artillery fire now homed in on the crossing site and pounded the area. The strong points and pockets of isolated German infantry, by-passed by the 1st Battalion, were now cleared by the 3rd Battalion and then it too moved off towards Korrenzig. By 1450hrs the whole of 334th Regiment was over the river.

Meanwhile the 1st battalion was keeping up the pressure and had moved on, by 1405hrs the battalion had advanced another 1,500 yards (1,365m) and taken Rurich. In less than 12 hours, the battalion had carved out a bridgehead 4,000 yards (3,640m) long by 1,000 yards (910m) deep. The next objective was Baal, 2,500 yards (2,275m) away to the north-east. The 3rd Battalion moved up and passed through the leading troops to take the town by 2115hrs that night, bumping into a German counter-attack on the way. At the end of the day two complete regiments were over the Roer, and occupied a bridgehead 3.5 miles (5.6km) long from Linnich to Baal, stretching down the river to the north-east. The German troops facing the 84th Division across the Roer were from the 59th Infantry Division (Poppe) and were disposed to

American 6 inch (155mm) Howitzer belonging to 113th Field Artillery Battalion from US 30th Infantry Division being towed across the River Roer on a floating pontoon bridge. The picture was taken on 24 February, the day after XIX Corps' assault crossing of the swollen river. (National Archives, Washington)

intercept an American crossing moving east towards the Rhine. In swinging north immediately after the crossing instead of due east where they were expected, the men of the 84th had outfoxed the enemy and turned things to their own advantage. The Americans also clashed with the inferior forces of the badly depleted 183rd Volksgrenadier Division (Lange) who were to the left of the German 59th Division.

South of Major-General Alexander Bolling's US 84th Division was 102nd Division, who crossed the Roer on the upstream side of Linnich. Major-General Frank Keating's 102nd Division formed the other part of XIII Corps' assault. Its crossing was launched after a deception plan using a diversionary smokescreen at an alternative site which drew away some of the German interdictory fire. Prior to the assault a raiding party under the command of Lt Roy Rogers went across the river and silenced four troublesome machine-gun posts. Minutes later the 407th Regiment's assault battalions followed across. The division's crossing was fairly uncomplicated and took few casualties. The villages of Gevenich and Tetz were taken that day, but the division had to withstand counter-attacks from both the German 59th Infantry Division and the 363rd Volksgrenadier Division (Dettling) backed by armour. The German attacks were repulsed with artillery and bazooka fire, there being no heavy weapons over the river at that time because of the lack of bridges.

Upstream from Linnich were the crossing sites allocated to McLain's XIX Corps. The most northerly, next to the 102nd Division, was MajGen Charles Gerhardt's 29th Division. It was due to cross in and above Jülich.

A party of VIPs in front of the Citadel at Jülich, just after they had taken lunch in the ruined fortress. From left to right: MajGen McLain (US XIX Corps), FM Montgomery (British 21st Army Group), Winston Churchill (British Prime Minister), MajGen Gillem (US XIII Corps), FM Brooke (British Chief Imperial Gen Staff) and LtGen Simpson (US 9th Army).
(Imperial War Museum)

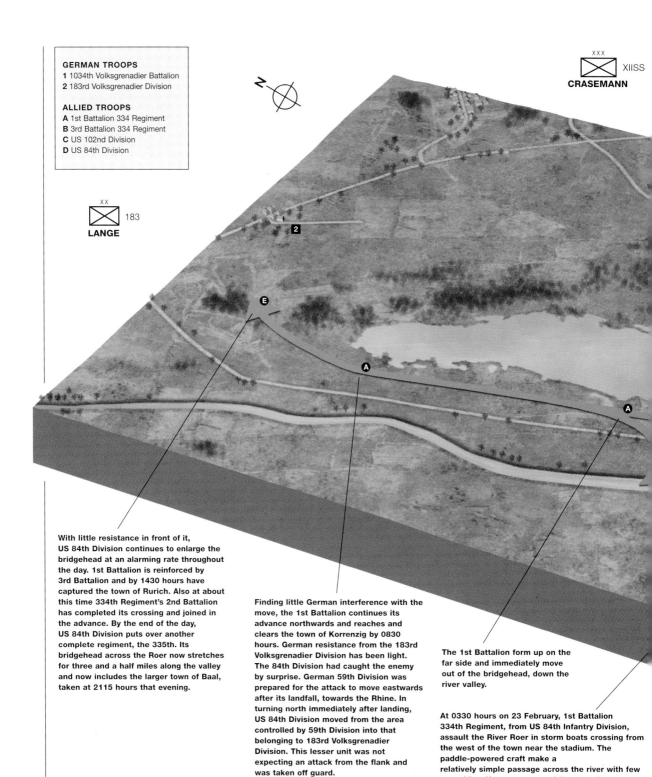

GERMAN TROOPS
1 1034th Volksgrenadier Battalion
2 183rd Volksgrenadier Division

ALLIED TROOPS
A 1st Battalion 334 Regiment
B 3rd Battalion 334 Regiment
C US 102nd Division
D US 84th Division

XXX
XIISS
CRASEMANN

XX
183
LANGE

2

E

A

A

With little resistance in front of it, US 84th Division continues to enlarge the bridgehead at an alarming rate throughout the day. 1st Battalion is reinforced by 3rd Battalion and by 1430 hours have captured the town of Rurich. Also at about this time 334th Regiment's 2nd Battalion has completed its crossing and joined in the advance. By the end of the day, US 84th Division puts over another complete regiment, the 335th. Its bridgehead across the Roer now stretches for three and a half miles along the valley and now includes the larger town of Baal, taken at 2115 hours that evening.

Finding little German interference with the move, the 1st Battalion continues its advance northwards and reaches and clears the town of Korrenzig by 0830 hours. German resistance from the 183rd Volksgrenadier Division has been light. The 84th Division had caught the enemy by surprise. German 59th Division was prepared for the attack to move eastwards after its landfall, towards the Rhine. In turning north immediately after landing, US 84th Division moved from the area controlled by 59th Division into that belonging to 183rd Volksgrenadier Division. This lesser unit was not expecting an attack from the flank and was taken off guard.

The 1st Battalion form up on the far side and immediately move out of the bridgehead, down the river valley.

At 0330 hours on 23 February, 1st Battalion 334th Regiment, from US 84th Infantry Division, assault the River Roer in storm boats crossing from the west of the town near the stadium. The paddle-powered craft make a relatively simple passage across the river with few casualties. However, many of the storm boats are lost while trying to bring them back to the near shore ready for the second wave.

US 84 DIVISION CROSS THE RIVER ROER AT LINNICH, 24 FEBRUARY 1945

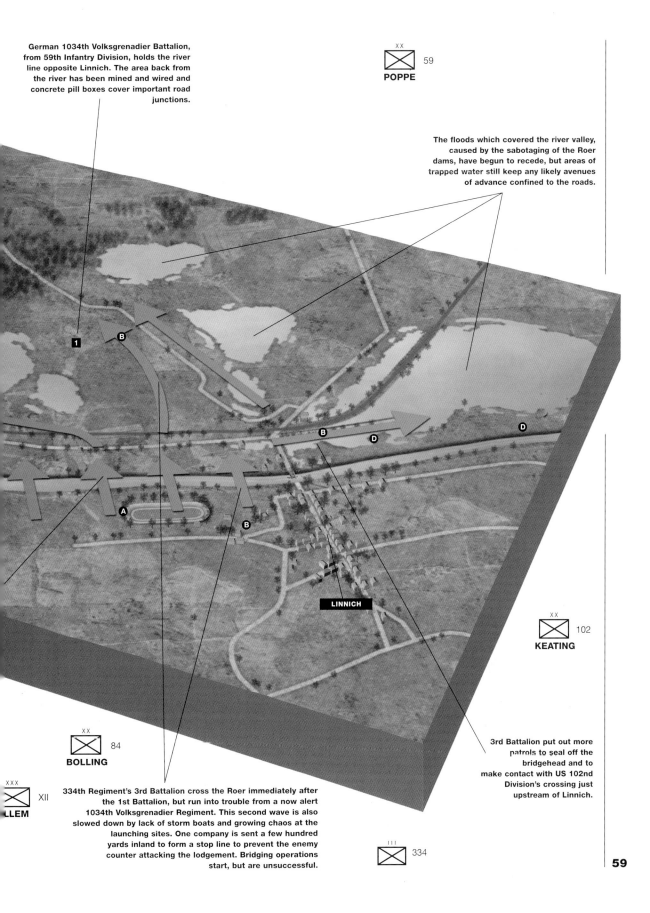

German 1034th Volksgrenadier Battalion, from 59th Infantry Division, holds the river line opposite Linnich. The area back from the river has been mined and wired and concrete pill boxes cover important road junctions.

The floods which covered the river valley, caused by the sabotaging of the Roer dams, have begun to recede, but areas of trapped water still keep any likely avenues of advance confined to the roads.

XX
59
POPPE

1

B

A

B

B

D

D

LINNICH

XX
102
KEATING

3rd Battalion put out more patrols to seal off the bridgehead and to make contact with US 102nd Division's crossing just upstream of Linnich.

XX
84
BOLLING

XXX
XII
LLEM

334th Regiment's 3rd Battalion cross the Roer immediately after the 1st Battalion, but run into trouble from a now alert 1034th Volksgrenadier Regiment. This second wave is also slowed down by lack of storm boats and growing chaos at the launching sites. One company is sent a few hundred yards inland to form a stop line to prevent the enemy counter attacking the lodgement. Bridging operations start, but are unsuccessful.

III
334

German troops captured by the US 102nd Division during the first day of 'Grenade'. The prisoners are all young men, some of them just boys, from the German 59th Division. The German division had suffered dreadful casualties in the previous fighting around Aachen and at one point was down to around 1,000 men. As with all German units, replacements were often just young boys or old men, conscripted into service with little equipment or training. They were often put into the line to help absorb an initial attack, before the more seasoned troops could be brought up to counter-attack any lodgement. (National Archives, Washington)

The river to the north of the town was too wide to bridge and the troops of 115th Infantry Regiment crossed over in assault boats and Landing Vehicle Tracked (LVTs). Just upstream in Jülich itself the river was much narrower with steep banks and the second assault regiment, 175th Regiment, crossed over on footbridges. An advance party had moved over the Roer to protect the sites whilst engineers built the bridges. When they were ready, the assaulting infantry raced across. Although casualties were heavier than elsewhere, they were still relatively light.

Dominating the town of Jülich was the Citadel, a 400-year-old fortress, with huge stone walls. Before the crossing, American bombers had plastered the fort with 1,000lb (450kg) bombs, but it had remained intact. Preparations were made to take the Citadel with tanks, explosives and flame-throwers but they were stranded on the western side of the river during day one. When they finally arrived over the river the next day, there was no costly assault to be endured for the Germans had withdrawn.

The most southerly of XIX Corps crossings was that carried out by the 30th Division, commanded by MajGen Leland Hobbs. Like the 29th Division, the 30th planned to cross dry shod. In fact it went one better, for an advance party of 119th Regiment went across an hour before the artillery bombardment began and provided a screen for engineers to start work on a footbridge. At the same time as the barrage went in, the engineers began building the bridge. By the time the last shells were falling, the regiment was racing across the completed bridge. The other assault unit was the 120th Regiment who crossed further upstream using LVTs.

Opposing XIX Corps was the 363rd Volksgrenadier Division. Its main offensive effort had been launched against 102nd Division downstream and it was unable to organise any counter-attacks against XIX Corps. The crossings had been completely successful with relatively slight casualties.

Not so the crossing in VII Corps' sector. General Collins' group had a much harder task in supporting the efforts of 9th Army. It assaulted the Roer with two divisions: MajGen Terry Allen's 104th Division on the left and MajGen William Weaver's 8th Division on the right, both in the area of Dueren. Collins divided the town between the two divisions. More than any of other crossings, the Roer at Düren proved to be the biggest problem during the D-Day of 'Grenade'. The swollen river running through its narrow course proved to be too swift for footbridges and all the infantry crossed in boats. In the 104th's area, the first waves of the 415th Regiment got across with little difficulty. The 413th Regiment had more trouble. Its first waves were almost completely wiped out as an effective force when it became disorganised by enemy counter fire. German artillery forced the remainder of the regiment to complete its crossing in the 415th's sector. By daylight, the German fire had made bridging operations almost impossible. Long-range artillery bombarded the sites all through the day. Smokescreens were laid but these had little effect, the guns were already registered on the bridge's locations. A direct hit completely demolished a finished road bridge. None the less, those troops over the river pressed inland and took two villages en route to Oberzier. Opposed by a weak 12th Volksgrenadier Division (Engel), the enemy failed to put up much resistance.

The final crossing, and the most southerly, was made by 8th Division. Crossing upstream of the 29th Division, this assault was the most precarious of them all. The crossing places were overlooked by the foothills of the Eifel and the enemy had the whole area registered by its artillery. The Roer was swift and narrow, with no possibility of bridges being built to get the first waves of troops across. All the assaults were made by boat; each of them was a disaster. The 13th and 28th Regiments were supposed to cross with powered assault boats, but virtually every one had engine malfunctions. Paddle-powered storm boats were too flimsy for the fast- flowing river and many of the craft tipped their loads of infantry into the icy waters. As the night became day, German fire increased in intensity limiting all operations on the river bank. Not one bridge was built during the day. Those troops that did make it over the river were disorganised and poorly equipped. Most of their weapons were lost during the crossing. Smashed by the river and pounded by the artillery, the 8th Division would have been an easy target, but the 12th Volksgrenadier Division never counter-attacked with any force.

Even with the problems suffered by VII Corps, the opening round of 'Grenade' could be viewed as a success. The 84th Division's penetration in the North and the lodgements gained by eight divisions had effectively broken the Roer as a defence line. The only real enemy counter-attack had been the one against 102nd Division. The great weight of American firepower and muscle would now inexorably pour across the river against a dispirited and increasingly emasculated opposition. Casualties had been light, the entire 9th Army had suffered 92 killed, 61 missing and 913 wounded, with the losses of VII Corps amounting to 66 killed, 35 missing and 280 wounded, a total of just under 1,500. It was a relatively small price to pay for such a large gain.

News of the American crossing of the Roer was received by Commander of Army Group B with some alarm. Generalfeldmarschall

OVERLEAF **In the early hours of a February morning the US 84th Division crossed the River Roer as part of Operation Grenade. Thirty-five storm boats were used in the first wave, but as they were paddle powered they crossed intermittently, with varying distances between them and at different speeds. The fast current tended to sweep them downstream and so their passing across the river was skewed, rather than straight. Enemy fire was sporadic and slight, but even so there were some casualties.**

Tank crewmen from
US 8th Armored Division help
medics lower an injured
infantryman from the rear of
their tank after having brought
him back to an aid station from
the front line. The tank is a
Sherman M4A3, it has the
larger .3 inch (76mm) gun
and horizontal volute spring
suspension. Picture taken at
Linne on 26 February 1945.
(National Archives, Washington)

Model acted swiftly and placed his reserves, the 9th and 11th Panzer Divisions, at the disposal of the German 15th Army's commander Von Zangen. Model had intended to use the two armoured divisions together as a corps under the command of GenLt Fritz Bayerlain, but not enough of the 11th Panzers had yet arrived from the Saar-Moselle sector where it had been deployed to justify the arrangement, so the divisions were handed over to Von Zangen. He, in turn, allocated those parts that were ready to move on to Koechling's LXXXI Corps. It was a mistake; this valuable armour dribbled into the battle rather than being thrown in as a powerful strike force.

Simpson's forces now turned to exploit the bridgehead. He was anxious to get his army pivoting to the north as early as possible. He knew that as each division wheeled to the left, its right wing would become vulnerable. It was absolutely imperative that everyone kept abreast of each other. XIX Corps was probably the most exposed in view of the trouble that VII Corps was having at its crossing sites.

The 84th Division led the way north clearing the far side of the Roer in order to allow Anderson's XVI Corps to cross unopposed. The division ran into trouble north of Baal and its advance slowed down. Simpson decided that, as opposition was comparatively light, Anderson should find and try to exploit his own crossing places rather than wait for XIII Corps to capture them for him. West of the Roer below Anderson were several German bridgeheads still on the Allied side of the Roer. Anderson now made to capture the one at Hilfarth, complete with the bridge across the river which was supplying the garrison in the town. He gave the task to 35th Division, while the 79th Division staged a feint several miles downstream. To assist the attack on Hilfarth, MajGen Baade

Five days into 'Grenade', infantrymen of the 2nd Battalion, 334th Regiment, from US 84th Division crouch in the shelter of an M3 half-rack personnel carrier to avoid enemy shrapnel and sniper fire. Resistance by this time consisted of small rearguards manning extemporised road blocks and setting ambushes to harry the advancing Americans with their small arms fire. (National Archives, Washington)

put 137th Regiment over the Roer into XIII Corps bridgehead to attack down the eastern side of the river. After a protracted fight, Hilfarth was captured with its bridge intact. By noon on 26 February tanks and other vehicles of XVI Corps now swarmed over the Roer in force, freeing up Gillem's XIII Corps to continue its advance northwards.

Gillem now inserted his 5th Armored Division onto his right flank and set the 84th and 102nd Divisions to take Erklenz and the last anti-tank ditch in front of the Americans. This they did against the feeble opposition put up by the German 338th Infantry Division (Von Oppen) which had just arrived into the sector controlled by XII SS Corps. With Erklenz captured the road network over a wide flat plain now opened up. It was perfect tank country. Now the advance began to gain momentum.

In front of XIX Corps, the introduction of elements of the 9th and 11th Panzer Divisions slowed the advance down, but the hurriedly committed German units could not put up a concerted defence, nor gain enough strength to counter-attack. The 29th and 30th Divisions now began to roll up this opposition between them. McLain then inserted his 2nd Armored Division to take over the lead and the advance motored on. XIX Corps' success was mirrored by Collins' VII Corps. After his sticky start at the river crossings, his troops applied 72 hours of unremitting pressure as successive fresh units went into the line to replace those tired by the fighting. It was too much for the 12th Volksgrenadier Division. Resistance collapsed leaving the bridgehead to expand at an alarming rate as the American corps headed east for the River Erft.

Simpson's army was now getting up to speed. His reserve divisions and armoured formations were introduced into the bridgehead and began to fan out, striking for important communication centres and river crossings. With the 84th Division still heading north, after taking Erklenz, and Anderson's corps pushing down the Roer valley, Model

German troops advance past a burning American half-track during the Ardennes offensive. Hitler's gamble, to attack through the mountainous region of Belgium in December 1944, was a failure and resulted in a great loss of men and matériel that could have been put to better use in the defence of the Reich within and behind the Siegfried Line. After this offensive, the depleted German Army in the west could only hope that a substantial stand against the advancing Allies could be made further back on the River Rhine. But Hitler would not even allow this and insisted that every metre of the ground between the German frontier and the river be defended to the last. By the time the front had been pushed back to the Rhine, there was very little left to defend it with.
(Imperial War Museum)

could detect that the possible direction of the attack was aimed at a link-up with the Canadian 1st Army and not eastwards towards Cologne and the Rhine as first supposed. If that were so, Von Zangen's 15th Army and the whole south wing of the German Army Group H was in danger of being caught in a great pincer movement and crushed. The Americans would then take Schlemm's II Parachute Army in the rear. Model informed his C-in-C West, Von Rundstedt, that it was no longer possible to form a defensive line on the east bank of the Rhine. Von Rundstedt consulted with Hitler and urged him to sanction a general retreat back across the Rhine; failure to do so, he warned, would lead to the collapse of the entire Western Front. Hitler dismissed the proposal outright. He even refused to agree to an adjustment to 15th Army's line. The fight to contain the Allies in the Rhineland would continue on its present course. To help prevent the collapse, Von Rundstedt ordered Blaskowitz to release the Panzer Lehr and 15th Panzer Grenadier Divisions to help bolster Von Zangen's defences. It was too little, too late.

The US 9th Army's great breakout made good use of its superiority over the Germans in mechanised warfare. The combination of armour and infantry in such large numbers was powerful enough to break any defence that the enemy was capable of mounting. Bill Simpson exercised a policy of 'relentless pursuit'. When the advance passed from the area controlled by the German 15th Army into that of the II Parachute Army, opposition became much tougher. Schlemm had withdrawn the German 8th Parachute Division from the Canadian sector and placed it in front of XVI Corps. The elite troops put up a dogged resistance whenever they could catch the Americans, but Simpson's leading groups often just by-passed the opposition, cut their rear and left the German defenders for the follow-up troops to deal with. Operation Grenade had become unstoppable.

THE FINAL BATTLE

In contrast to the light opposition encountered and breathtaking gains made by the US 9th Army in the South, the Canadian/British attack in the North continued unabated. Crerar's Army was locked into a battle that had little real scope for mobile warfare until the stubborn defences of the Westwall had been broken. He had to ask his troops for one more great effort and to suffer even more attrition until the Rhine was reached.

On the right of the battleground, XXX Corps advanced along two axes: Gennep–Venlo and Goch–Geldern. The 51st Highland Division had helped in the capture of Goch and was now engaged in crossing the small River Kendal, a tributary of the Niers, south of the town. On 25 February the division crossed the river and took its final objective, a lateral road heading south-east towards Weeze. The 51st Highland Division was then pulled out of the line and sent back to the rear for rest and refitting. It had been earmarked by Montgomery for the proposed Rhine crossings. The 52nd Lowland Division took over the sector held by the Highland Division and continued southwards, clearing the east bank of the Maas.

Men from the 1st Battalion Herefordshire Regiment cross the anti-tank ditch that surrounds Udem. The ditches were a common type of temporary defence which were thrown up throughout the whole of the Siegfried Line. They caused little difficulty to the infantry and could be bridged in seconds with specialised armoured bridging equipment. Covering fire, smoke and a determined attack meant that troops and tanks could be over the ditch in a very short space of time. The secret was in trying to keep the enemy occupied whilst the breach was made.
(Imperial War Museum)

LEFT AND BELOW **On the day, 3 March, that the Welsh Division joined up with the US 35th Division at Geldern, completing the linking of the 'Veritable' and 'Grenade' offensives, the Royal Norfolks of the British 3rd Division were capturing the town of Kervenheim, to the left of the Welshmen. The pictures show infantry street fighting and clearing houses in the town. (Imperial War Museum)**

RIGHT **The parish church and stone tower of Goch suffered from the Allied bombardment during the capture of the town. The tower had been standing since the 14th century, but this did not escape its being plastered with a 'Hitler Youth' sign an each of its walls. The picture was taken on 3 March, just a few days after the town's capture by the Scottish and Highland Divisions. (Imperial War Museum)**

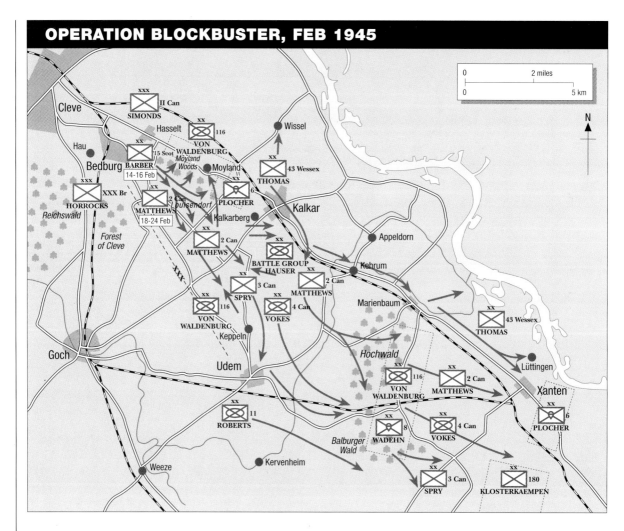

OPERATION BLOCKBUSTER, FEB 1945

After its welcome release from the confines of the Reichswald and a few days' rest out of the line, the 53rd Welsh Division led the advance from Goch to Geldern. The three towns of Weeze, Kevelaer and Geldern to its front were all fortified. On the left of 53rd Division, the 15th Scottish Division advanced abreast of it for a few more days until it too was relieved by a fresh division. On 25 February the British 3rd Division commanded by MajGen 'Bolo' Whistler crossed the River Maas and took over the sector in front of the Scottish Division, resuming the advance two days later.

Meanwhile the 53rd Division pressed on. The ground was still littered with anti-tank ditches, barbed-wire and concrete fortifications, but the pressure applied by XXX Corps' three divisions was constant and resolute. Weeze fell to the Welshmen in a two-brigade pincer attack, while Kevelaer followed soon after on 2 March, when reconnaissance troops found the town to be unoccupied. The next town, Geldern, was to be the pivot for a change of direction. Once the town had been captured, XXX Corps would swing to the east and head for the bridges at Wesel, meeting up with the Canadians and sealing those German troops that were encircled in the trap. Geldern was also to be the meeting place with the Americans racing up from the south aiming to complete an even greater encirclement.

After XXX Corps had broken up the western side of the battlefield with its capture of Goch, it became the turn of the Canadian II Corps to attack in the East. The corps had been badly mauled when trying to capture the Moyland woods and advance over the Goch–Calcar road and it took a few days to rethink tactics and plan for a new offensive. Crerar decided to add weight to his forces and plan a heavy thrust through the line of fortifications known as the 'Hochwald Layback' which barred the way to Xanten and the Rhine. Instead of advancing with the Cleve–Xanten road as his axis, he planned to take his main force round the south of Calcar and head across the high ground through the gap between the Hochwald Forest and the smaller Balbergerwald, approaching Xanten from west of the town. Once Xanten was captured, Wesel and the bridges over the Rhine were doomed. Xanten was the gateway to the Rhine.

Crerar's troops would be attacking one of the strongest sections of the Rhine defences. General Schlemm had ordered his two corps commanders in the area, Von Luttwitz and Meindl, to reinforce the escarpment that stretched from Calcar to Udem. This ridge of high ground barred the way through the gap south of the Hochwald. Behind the ridge were further tank ditches, pillboxes and wire entanglements. The gap itself was covered by a remarkable number of .3 inch (88mm) guns, salvaged from the Siegfried Line defences.

A German infantry unit command post, overrun by the US 1st Army during the breakout to the Rhine. The camouflaged field HQ is set into the ground with wooden sides and roof giving overhead cover. (National Archives, Washington)

Hot food is unloaded from a mess truck at Wegburg onto a jeep to be taken up to the forward troops of the US 8th Armored Division on 2 March. Progress by the division had been through relatively undefended country, but from this point onwards the 8th Armored, from US XVI Corps, was to come up against the Germans facing the Canadian 1st Army and resistance to its advance stiffened alarmingly. (National Archives, Washington)

The operation was given the name 'Blockbuster'. Simonds had been loaned the British 43rd Infantry and 11th Armoured Divisions to help with the assault. On 26 February, just as the American forces over the Roer had got into their stride, the Canadians attacked. Two infantry divisions, the Canadian 2nd and 3rd, crossed the start line on the Goch–Calcar road and began sweeping the enemy aside. Carried in Kangaroo armoured troop carriers and moving at a brisk tank pace, the infantry advanced behind a rolling barrage. It was not long before they met stiffer opposition as Gen Schlemm's parachute forces began to make their presence felt. Support came from the Canadian 4th Armored Division, commanded by MajGen Chris Vokes, and Udem was taken after a bitter struggle. The axis of the attack then swung eastwards and the Canadians made for the Hochwald Gap, with the 2nd Canadian Division attacking the Hochwald on the left, the 3rd Canadian Division the Balbergerwald on the right and the 4th Canadian Armored Division plunging straight through the middle. This is where the whole offensive came to a shuddering halt. The ground was too exposed, and the enemy too firmly ensconced, for the Canadians to brush the opposition aside.

It took the Canadians five days to break through the gap and the woods. Five days of murderous and costly fighting in conditions that matched the worst days of the war. On the left flank the 43rd Division made an easier advance through Calcar and headed for Xanten down the main road, opposition becoming lighter all the way as German troops pulled back into Xanten lest they be surrounded. To the south of the Balbergerwald, the British 11th Armoured Division joined in the fight and added their weight to the advance. On 2 March, the Canadian II Corps successfully broke through the woods and looked down on Xanten, the last town before the Rhine.

To the south momentous events were unfolding. Simpson's 9th Army was sweeping all before it. Anderson's XVI Corps was pushing down the Maas, closing on the British XXX Corps; Gillem's XIII Corps was wheeling north-east to Krefeld and the Rhine; and McLain's XIX Corps had captured Mönchengladbach, the largest German town to fall so far in the war, and was now plunging eastwards making for the Rhine opposite Düsseldorf. The right flank protection, given by Collins' VII Corps, had expanded into a full-blown advance, having itself joined in the charge and crossed the River Erft, and now bore down on the great city of Cologne. Von Zangen's 15th Army could do little to stop them.

On 3 March, the British XXX Corps' 53rd Welsh Division, together with the 8th Armoured Brigade, continued their advance towards Geldern. Just after midday they met up with the US 35th Division just outside the town; 'Veritable' and 'Grenade' had finally joined together to provide a continuous front. The fate of the Germans west of the lower Rhine was now sealed. British XXX Corps, Canadian II Corps and the American XVI Corps all began heading east for the river, squeezing the enemy into a rapidly diminishing bridgehead. Elements of 15 German divisions were backing up to the Rhine, caught in the vice of the advancing Allied armies. Schlemm pleaded with Von Rundstedt to allow him to withdraw what was left of the 1st Parachute Army over the river,

Knocked-out Sturmpanzer VI (Sturmtiger) assault gun, one of only ten built, being examined by an infantryman from the US 30th Infantry Division. The Sturmtiger housed a 15 inch (380mm) rocket projector, intended for use as a mobile assault howitzer against troop concentrations and fortifications. The picture was taken on 28 February 1945, five days into US 9th Army's advance. (National Archives, Washington)

but Hitler still blocked the move. On 5 March the Americans finally reached the Rhine further to the south and one by one the bridges across the river were blown to prevent them falling into Allied hands.

The remnants of the II Parachute Army were gradually squeezed into a tiny lodgement around the two remaining Rhine bridges at Wesel. By 6 March Schlemm began evacuating some of his troops across the road and rail crossings, in defiance of orders, but he still maintained his vigorous defence of the 'pocket' around Wesel. When the Canadians and the 43rd Division attacked Xanten after a terrific barrage, they still found a determined and tenacious German garrison defending the town. The Americans also found to their great cost just what the Canadian 1st Army had had to contend with when they too met stiff German resistance from the paratroopers holding the Wesel 'pocket'. After the rapid advance from the Roer, the last few miles to the Rhine were some of the most difficult met by the Americans during the whole of the journey.

On 3 March 1945 at around 3pm the British and the Americans met near the canal just outside the small town of Geldern. The British had driven south as part of Operation Veritable, whilst the Americans, as part of Operation Grenade, had pushed north to meet the Anglo-Canadian units. This encounter helped seal the retreating enemy into a pocket with their backs to the River Rhine.

By 8 March the Germans knew that to hold out any longer was pointless. Under strict orders from Hitler not to allow the bridges to fall into Allied hands on pain of death, Gen Schlemm pulled back into Wesel all who could be released to do so. With just a few dogged defenders keeping the advancing Allied armies at bay, everything that could be moved was saved, but masses of equipment had to be abandoned. The end came on 10 March when both bridges at Wesel crashed into the river, leaving just a brave rearguard and a few stragglers to be mopped up by the Americans and British. The butcher's bill for the German campaign to stop the British 21st Army was over 90,000 men. Allied losses amounted to 22,934, of which 7,300 were American, 5,304 Canadian and 10,330 were British. It was the last great stand-up fight between the Germans and the Allies; the rest of the war for the Nazi regime was marked by a long retreat into oblivion.

Tony Bryan 04/00

THE AMERICAN DRIVE TO THE RHINE

Whilst Montgomery's British 21st Army Group struggled with its epic campaign in the north of Germany, Bradley's 12th Army Group and Devers' 6th Army Group continued Eisenhower's 'broad front' policy and were steadily pushing the enemy back to the River Rhine all along the line.

Bradley's initial moves in early February were a continuation of the clearing of the 'bulge' formed by Hitler's Ardennes offensive of December 1944. He knew that the main thrust was to be in the north, but sought Eisenhower's permission to carry on through the Eifel region in an attempt to capitalise on the disorganised German retreat from the Ardennes. Eisenhower gave the go-ahead providing that such an advance resulted in a quick and decisive penetration of the enemy's defences, followed by a rapid drive to the Rhine. Eisenhower warned Bradley not to get bogged down in the mountainous fir-covered forests of the Eifel.

The elimination of the German penetration in the Ardennes had pushed back the German 6th Panzer Army to a point that it was pulled out of the line by Hitler and sent to the Eastern Front. That left the German 5th Panzer and 7th Armies facing Bradley, both of which had been badly mauled during the winter offensive. The German High Command could not believe that the Americans would attack through the Eifel in winter and decided to move some of its strength northwards opposite Simpson's

American troops pass a knocked-out M24 light tank that had been disabled by armour-piercing shot during a German ambush just short of the Rhine.
(National Archives, Washington)

Three 15-year-old soldiers taken prisoner by the US 1st Army's 9th Infantry Division at Siptenfelde. The fresh-faced youths appeared to be none the worse for their ordeal. (National Archives, Washington)

9th Army, where they thought an attack would be more likely. This decision led to the shuffling of units opposite Bradley's sector and gave him more confidence that the Eifel was just the place through which to launch his attack. He could not have been more wrong.

On 28 January, Hodges' 1st Army and Patton's 3rd Army advanced into the frontier defences north-east of St. Vith. The going was very slow. It was not so much the enemy in the shape of the German 5th Panzer Army that stalled them, as the weather. The American divisions that launched the attack had to contend with waist-high snow drifts, icy roads, frozen equipment and overcast skies. Movement was slow and precarious; traffic jams and treacherous conditions held progress to a crawl. In the first few days of the advance, the three American corps that undertook the attack had only managed to draw up to the first pillboxes of the Siegfried Line. On 1 February, Eisenhower called a halt to the proceedings and ordered Bradley to release seven divisions to 9th Army to help in Montgomery's offensive. He also gave instructions for the capture of the Roer dams as 1st Army's main priority.

While Bradley's main advance was halted, there was a problem in the south of his sector that required immediate attention. The enemy still held a triangle of land between the Saar and Moselle rivers near Trier that needed to be eliminated. General George Patton's 3rd Army was given the task to clear the area and bring the American line up to the defences of the Westwall. Again, it was bitter fighting in bitter winter weather. The task took the form of successive limited objective attacks culminating in one all-out attack by the 3rd Army on 19 February before the German forces could be eliminated from the triangle.

Still farther south, in the sector controlled by Devers' 6th Army Group, an American-French attack eliminated the German bridgehead across the Rhine known as the 'Colmar Pocket', on 9 February. The combined attack by US 7th Army and French 1st Army pushed Balck's 19th Army back across the river. This brought Allied forces up to the west bank of the Rhine all the way from Strasbourg to the Swiss border. The fighting cost the French and Americans 18,000 casualties; the Germans probably suffered double that number.

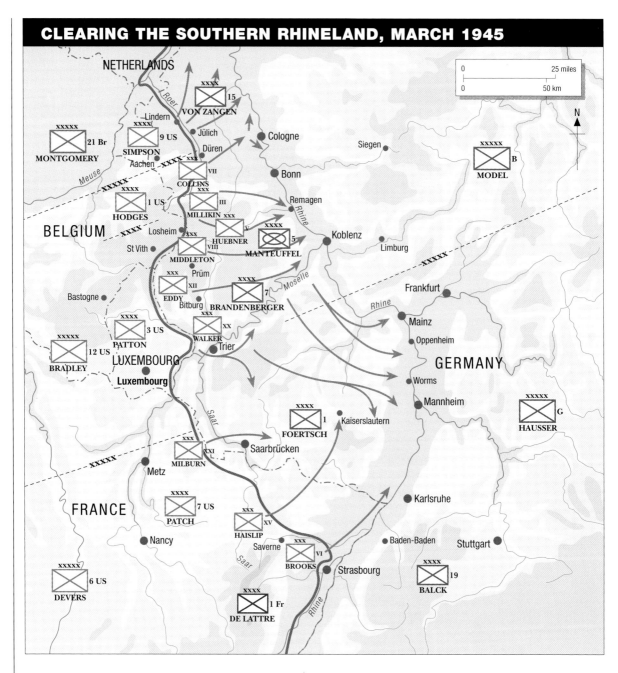

Even though Bradley had had to relinquish nine divisions to Simpson and Montgomery, his 12th Army Group was still a considerable striking force. After the commencement of 'Grenade' Bradley was able to contemplate his general move to the Rhine, code-named 'Lumberjack'. Gen Collins' US VII Corps had already attacked across the River Roer in support of US 9th Army's Operation Grenade. It now became the lead corps for 1st Army's drive to the Rhine, gathering momentum as the 'Grenade' campaign developed. Hodges used the bridgehead created by VII Corps to insert other units into the battle zone. Rather than stage assault crossings of their own, Hodges introduced one division after another each using the bridges of the adjacent division, then shifting

south to create other bridging sites for other divisions. US III Corps, under the command of MajGen John Millikin, crossed over VII Corps' bridges before moving south to create sites for the next corps, V Corps, under MajGen Heubner. As Collins' VII Corps reached the city of Cologne it turned south down the Rhine to link up with III Corps. Millikin's corps in turn moved south-east to meet the confluence of the Rivers Ahr and Rhine, to join up with the leading elements of Patton's 3rd Army who were attacking eastwards from the area of the Eifel. With the severe winter weather gradually easing, Patton's men had managed to seize the two main road centres in the western Eifel – Prüm and Bitberg – and had driven east to the River Kyle.

The American armies were now gradually breaking out of the confines of the Westwall. The shifting of troops to the North had weakened German resistance to a point where it was rapidly becoming disorganised. The northern wing of Von Zangen's German 15th Army had been shattered by Simpson's advance and the eastwards drive by Collins. Further south, Hodges' and Patton's moves through the southern Eifel had added to Model's woes by smashing through the German 5th Panzer Army (Manteuffel) and the German 7th Army, now commanded by Gen der Infanterie Hans Felber. In addition, Patton's drive down the Moselle valley was putting pressure on the German 1st Army and unhinging the whole of the German Army Group G and the industrial area of the Saar.

On 3 March, just as VII Corps had reached the Rhine north of Cologne, Patton's 3rd Army made its strike: Troy Middleton's VIII Corps headed eastwards from Prum and MajGen Manton Eddy's XII Corps crossed the River Kyle east of Bitburg. The going was slow at first, especially near Prüm as the enemy struggled to contain the assault, but on 5 March, Patton unleashed his armour and by nightfall they had advanced over 12 miles (19.3km). The tanks moved against negligible opposition – Manteuffel's 5th Panzer Army could do little to stop them – cutting through hastily organised strong points and heading straight for the Rhine. In just over two-and-a-half days, the US 4th Armored

Division had advanced 44 miles (70km), taking over 5,000 prisoners and spreading alarm and confusion in the German rear. Everywhere, German troops were pulling back on foot, in horse-drawn carts and in commandeered motor vehicles, searching for crossing points over the Rhine whether they be barges, bridges or ferries. One by one the bridges over the Rhine were blown as Hodges' and Patton's forces neared the river. Each German commander knew that the penalty for allowing a bridge to fall into Allied hands was death. But, on 7 March, a catalogue of German mishaps, exploited by brave and determined American troops, allowed elements of MajGen John Leonard's 9th Armored Division from Millikin's III Corps to capture the Remagen bridge intact, although it was severely damaged. A bridgehead was quickly put over the river and reinforced in strength over the next few days. The bridge finally collapsed into the river ten days later, but by then several alternative crossing sites had been established.

No sooner had Patton's forces reached the Rhine than they turned swiftly southwards, sweeping up the valley to get behind the troops of the German 7th and 1st Armies who were manning the Westwall facing Patch's US 7th Army. GenObst Paul Hausser, commander Army Group G, realised that unless reinforcements could be sent to bolster the German 7th Army against Patton, his 1st Army would be surrounded and annihilated. The reply that came from the new Commander-in-Chief West, GFM Albert Kesselring (who had replaced the disgraced Von Rundstedt), was that no reinforcements were available. On 12 March Patton attacked from Trier with XX Corps (Walker), whilst XII Corps (Eddy) crossed the Moselle near the Rhine and drove south-west into the rear of the German 1st Army. Gen Foertsch, the German 1st Army's commander, was gradually being enveloped, for as Patton harried the rear, Patch and De Lattre pounded his front with their US 7th and French 1st Armies. Once again Hausser appealed to Kesselring, this time to be allowed to pull his forces back across the Rhine. Permission was denied, but Kesselring did suggest that any American encirclement that threatened the annihilation of the main body of troops was to be avoided. This was no authority for a full-scale withdrawal, but it was enough of a hint to allow the most seriously threatened units to be pulled back.

The American armies now operated through open country against only sporadic resistance. On 20 March permission was given to Felber to pull his German 7th Army back over the Rhine, while the remnants of German 1st Army held bridgeheads around the three remaining bridges. On 23 March, approval was finally issued for a formal withdrawal across the river. By that time almost all who were going to make it back had already done so. At the end of the next day the last Rhine bridge crashed into the river and only stragglers and abandoned equipment were left on the west bank. The River Rhine, from the North Sea to the Swiss border, now marked the Allied front line.

AFTERMATH

To the Germans the River Rhine was the last shield before the Ruhr and the last practical defensive line before the great north German plain. It was also a great psychological barrier for the German nation. Once it was crossed and the Allies were pouring out into the Nazi Fatherland, every person would, in their hearts, know that the war was lost.

By the end of March 1945, British, Canadian, American and French forces were all lined up along the whole length of the Rhine and their commanders were contemplating how best to cross the great German moat. Even though the Americans had their bridgehead over the river at Remagen, the area on the far side was not suitable for immediate large- scale operations. The Remagen lodgement would be exploited, but until it could be expanded and developed to contain a powerful striking force, it was much more of a symbolic breach of the Rhine than a practical one.

The main effort was once again in the north where Montgomery, true to form, took his 21st Army Group across the Rhine in a ponderous, set-piece, assault supported by air landings on the far side. The crossings, code-named 'Plunder', were an extension of his Rhineland campaign. Montgomery had been conditioned by the harsh opposition he had received in the February/March battles and was intent on ensuring that his overwhelming fighting power was put to good effect. 'Plunder' was heavily supported by air strikes, smoke and artillery on a massive scale. On 24 March, the British 2nd and US 9th Armies, under the command

An American machine-gun crew of the 102nd Division manning a .3 inch (76mm) Browning Model 1917 medium machine gun in a captured factory at Uerdingen. The gun first entered service in 1918 during World War I and remained in use in the American army until the early 1960s. (National Archives, Washington)

of LtGen Miles Dempsey and LtGen Bill Simpson, were put over onto the far side of the Rhine either side of Wesel and quickly established strong bridgeheads. The British moved north-east onto the northern plain, as the Americans began a wide south-easterly encirclement of the Ruhr industrial region.

In contrast to Montgomery, the other American armies chose to improvise their crossing and exploit any tactical situation as it occurred. With US 1st Army already across the river at Remagen, Patton's 3rd Army quickly followed suit at Nierstein when his 5th Division, from XII Corps, jumped the river one day before Monty's set-piece attack. Other crossings swiftly followed: on the 25th the US 87th Division crossed at Boppard and the 89th Division at St. Goar. A day later US 7th Army got across the river at Worms and even the French soon got into the act with their crossing at Gamersheim. In just a few days, the whole of the Rhine barrier had been breached.

Allied forces now fanned out and split the Germans apart. Montgomery's armies drove through Blaskowitz's German Army Group B with the Canadians heading for northern Holland, whilst 2nd Army made for Bremen and Hamburg. Simpson's 9th Army continued its envelopment of the Ruhr to meet up with Hodges' 1st Army and seal the German defenders of Model's 5th Panzer Army in an iron ring. Model's other two armies, the 15th and the 7th, were split wide open by the remaining forces of US 1st Army. Eisenhower then decreed that the main Allied thrust would be by Bradley's armies for the city of Leipzig and that Berlin, always the great objective of the British, was to be left for the Russians to capture. In consequence, Simpson's 9th Army reverted back to Bradley and the giant part of the capture of the remainder of Germany was given over to the Americans. Patton cleared the southern part of the country and moved into Czechoslovakia, Patch swept through Nuremberg and over the Austrian border, and De Lattre de Tassingy took his French 1st Army through the Black Forest, up into the Tyrol.

That these lightning moves were possible was in no small measure due to the Russians. The opposition was disorganised. Hitler was fighting a war on two fronts and the numbers of men involved in the East almost

dwarfed the Anglo-American operations in the west. The war with Russia was on a massive scale. At the end of 1944 the Red Army had gained a foothold in East Prussia, but then paused in order to build up strength for their final offensive. The Germans did all they could to improvise defences and tried desperately to amass enough units to counter the expected blow, but when it came the attack was of such massive power and ferocity that the Eastern Front, like the Western, was torn wide open. Over a million-and-a-half Russian troops faced just a third of that number of Germans on the East Prussian front alone. The amount of armour at their disposal was equally overwhelming: 3,000 Russian tanks against 700 German. The January offensive drove a deep bulge in the German line and got to within 60 miles (96km) of Berlin. The penetration was then exploited to the full during the campaigns in Silesia and Pomerania during February and March and the front line was gradually pushed back all along the German mainland.

The battles of March and April broke out everywhere and were conducted by everyone. All of the Allies, both in the west and the east harried the Germans at every opportunity. The German collapse, when it came, was total and final. On 30 April Hitler committed suicide in his Berlin bunker; on 4 May German forces in north-west Europe surrendered to the Allies.

THE BATTLEFIELD TODAY

The battles for control of the Rhineland took place in a heavily populated western nation and brought great devastation to its towns and cities. It is therefore only natural that after the war Germany began the great task of rebuilding itself and totally obliterating the permanent reminders of its unhappy past. Virtually every one of the ferro-concrete structures that made up Hitler's great Westwall have been destroyed, most of them by American engineers within days or even hours of their capture, fearful lest they fall once again into German hands. Others became eyesores or were in the way of progress or redevelopment and were removed. Some still exist, tucked away in isolated woods, or built into the side of a hill and overgrown with vegetation, but too few remain to illustrate the power of the Siegfried Line. In a few places, most notably around Aachen, sections of 'dragon's teeth' still survive, marching across fields as if waiting to trap some unsuspecting tank.

The temporary field works, dug in desperation as the Allies approached, disappeared immediately after the war when returning German farmers reclaimed their land and put it to good use helping to feed the nation. There is one notable exception, however, for at the base of the escarpment, just one mile to the north of Goch, the first of the anti-tank ditches dug to protect the town remains intact. Still 20 feet (6m) deep and covered with saplings, it rests at the foot of the low hill so brilliantly captured by the 43rd Wessex Division in the action which turned 'Veritable'.

All of the towns devastated in the battles have been rebuilt, but there are just enough of the original buildings showing scars of the war to recreate the past. It is possible to relive the battle in one's mind as you stand with some action photograph and compare what was then with what is now. At Linnich, just below the rebuilt bridge you can look down on the crossing site of the US 84th Division where its leading troops stormed across the Roer at the opening of 'Grenade', the river unchanged in over 50 years.

Well away from the roads, in areas seldom visited by anyone, you can still come across a long-forgotten battlefield. Slit trenches and dugouts, abandoned as the battle moved on, remain just as they were left, with the accumulation of 50 years of leaves falling into their open sides. The area in front of the trenches is often littered with cartridge cases, buried just 2 inches (50mm) below the surface lying just where they fell, spinning from a soldier's rifle. But perhaps the most evocative site of all is the deep forest of the Reichswald, where the British XXX Corps fought its terrible battle. The thick woods, intersected by long straight rides, remain just as they were. In the winter, in the rain, with mud underfoot and grey skies overhead, it's just as though you were back in the dark days of 1945.

RIGHT **After 24 hours without rest, these two tankers from the US 2nd Armored Division warm their feet by a fire. BrigGen I. D. White's division was part of McLain's XIX Corps, on the right flank of Gen Simpson's US 9th Army. The 2nd Armored Division led the advance with little respite once the corps had broken out from the Roer crossings.**
(National Archives, Washington)

CHRONOLOGY

1944

19 November US 9th Army attacks Hitler's Westwall defences (Siegfried Line) and reaches the River Roer.

16 December Hitler launches his great offensive through the Ardennes in an attempt to reach the River Meuse and split the British and American armies.

1945

12 January Russian Red Army launch their great winter offensive against the East German front.

16 January The Ardennes offensive fails and the German forces who had undertaken the attack are forced back to their original start line. The 'bulge' in the American front had been eliminated.

28 January US 1st and 3rd Armies start to move eastwards towards the Rhine through the Eifel region but are halted by Eisenhower three days later due to lack of progress against the Westwall defences.

1 February British XII Corps clears Roermond Triangle to bring Allied forces up to River Maas.

8 February Canadian 1st Army launches Operation Veritable with attacks through and around the Reichswald Forest.

11 February Canadian 1st Army takes the important town of Cleve in the heart of the Westwall defences.

9 February US 6th Army eliminates Colmar 'Pocket' and closes on the upper Rhine.

10 February US 1st Army captures Roer dams, but Germans flood the valley preventing the start of US 9th Army's Operation Grenade.

17 February The 43rd Wessex Division advances to the Goch escarpment and produce an 8,000 yard (7,280m) salient through the Siegfried Line which outflanks the Reichswald defences.

22 February 15th Scottish and 51st Highland Divisions take the town of Goch and finally break through Hitler's Westwall.

23 February US 9th Army begins 'Grenade' and cross the River Roer.

26 February US XVI Corps crosses the River Roer at Hilfarth and sweep down the eastern side of the River Maas towards the Canadian 1st Army.

26 February General Crerar launches Operation Blockbuster with Canadian II Corps in an attempt to break through the 'Hochwald Layback' and take Xanten to reach the Rhine opposite Wesel.

1 March US 9th Army captures Mönchengladbach.

3 March XVI Corps of US 9th Army and British XXX Corps of Canadian 1st Army link up at Geldern to complete the joining of 'Veritable' and 'Grenade'.

7 March US III Corps captures Rhine bridge intact at Remagen and establish a bridgehead for US 1st Army.

10 March Final two bridges at Wesel are blown by the Germans and British 21 Army completes its clearance of west bank of northern Rhine.

14 March US 3rd Army crosses lower River Moselle to outflank Siegfried Line.

22/23 March US 3rd Army crosses Rhine near Nierstein.

23 March Approval given by Hitler for a formal withdrawal across the Rhine of all German forces, but by that time all who were going to make it back had already gone.

23/24 March British 21st Army Group crosses Rhine as part of Operation Plunder.

24/25 March British and American airborne forces land east of the Rhine to link up with British 21st Army Group.

31 March French 1st Army crosses Rhine near Germersheim.

ORDERS OF BATTLE
FEBRUARY 1945

German Army

Commander-in-Chief (West) – Gerd von Rundstedt

Army Group H (Blaskowitz)

25th Army (Von Blumentritt)

XXX Corps (Fretter-Pico)

346 Infantry Division (Steinmueller)

6 Parachute Division (Plocher)

LXXXVIII Corps (Reinhard)

2 Parachute Division (Lackner)

1st Parachute Army (Schlemm)

LXXXVI Corps (Straube)

180 Infantry Division (Klosterkemper)

190 Infantry Division (Hammer)

II Parachute Corps (Meindl)

7 Parachute Division (Erdmann)

8 Parachute Division (Wadehn)

84 Infantry Division (Feibig)

XLVII Corps (von Luttwitz)

15 Panzer Grenadier Division (Maucke)

116 Panzer Division (Von Waldenburg)

Army Group B (Model)

15th Army (von Zangen)

XII SS Corps (Crasemann)

59 Infantry Division (Poppe)

176 Infantry Division (Landau)

183 Infantry Division (Lange)

LXXXI Corps (Koechling)

12 Volksgrenadier Division (Engel)

363 Volksgrenadier Division (Dettling)

353 Infantry Division (Thieme)

5th Panzer Army (Manteuffel)

LXXIV Corps (Puechler)

85 Infantry Division (Chill)

62 Volksgrenadier Division (Kittel)

272 Volksgrenadier Division (Konig)

3 Parachute Division (Schimpf)

3 Panzer Grenadier Division (Denkert)

9 Panzer Division (Von Elverfeldt)

LXVII Corps (Hitzfeld)

26 Volksgrenadier Division (Kocott)

89 Infantry Division (Bruns)

277 Volksgrenadier Division (Viebig)

LXVI Corps (Lucht)

18 Volksgrenadier Division (Hoffmann-Schonborn)

246 Volksgrenadier Division (Korte)

326 Volksgrenadier Division (Kaschner)

2 Panzer Division (Kokott)

5 Parachute Division (Heilmann)

7th Army (Brandenberger)

XIII Corps (Felber)

167 Volksgrenadier Division (Hocker)

276 Volksgrenadier Division (Dempwolff)

340 Volksgrenadier Division (Tolsdorf)

LIII Corps (Rothkirch und Trach)

9 Volksgrenadier Division (Kolb)

79 Volksgrenadier Division (Hummel)

352 Volksgrenadier Division (Bazing)

LXXX Corps (Beyer)

212 Volksgrenadier Division (Sensfuss)

560 Volksgrenadier Division (Langhauser)

Army Group G (Hausser)

1st Army (Foertsch)

LXXXII Corps (Hahm)

416 Infantry Division (Pflieger)

11 Panzer Division (Wietersheim)

LXXXV Corps (Kniess)

347 Infantry Division (Trierenberg)

719 Infantry Division (Gade)

XIII SS Corps (Von Oriola)

19 Volksgrenadier Division (Britzelmayr)

559 Volksgrenadier Division (Von Muhlen)

17 SS Panzer Grenadiers (Klingenberg)

XC Corps (Peterson)

6 SS Division (Brenner)

36 Volksgrenadier Division (Welln)

LXXXIV Corps (Behlendorff)

47 Volksgrenadier Division (Bork)

257 Volksgrenadier Division (Seidel)

553 Volksgrenadier Division (Huter)

19th Army (Balck)

XVIII SS Corps (Meyer)

405 Replacement Division (Seeger)

708 Volksgrenadier Division (Bleckwenn)

LXIII Corps (Abraham)

16 Volksgrenadier Division (Haeckel)

159 Infantry Division (Burcky)

189 Infantry Division (Bauer)

198 Infantry Division (Schiel)

338 Infantry Division (Von Oppen)

NOTE: The overall situation on the Western Front in early 1945 was chaotic and meant that many of the above German units were incomplete, often only existed in battle groups and were being shifted from sector to sector at short notice. It would be very difficult to give an exact German 'order of battle' on any front at this period of the war.

Allied Armies

Supreme Allied Commander – Dwight D. Eisenhower.

US 12th Army Group (Bradley)
- US XVIII Airborne Corps (Ridgway)
  - US 17 Airborne Division (Miley)
  - US 82 Airborne Division (Gavin)
  - US 101 Airborne Division (Taylor)
- US 1st Army (Hodges)
  - US III Corps (Millikin)
    - US 1 Infantry Division (Andrus)
    - US 9 Infantry Division (Craig)
    - US 78 Infantry Division (Parker)
    - US 9 Armored Division (Leonard)
  - US V Corps (Heubner)
    - US 2 Infantry Division (Robertson)
    - US 28 Infantry Division (Cota)
    - US 69 Infantry Division (Reinhardt)
    - US 106 Infantry Division (Perrin)
    - US 7 Armored Division (Hasbruck)
  - US VII Corps (Collins)
    - US 8 Infantry Division (Weaver)
    - US 104 Infantry Division (Allen)
    - US 3 Armored Division (Rose)
    - US 99 Infantry Division (Lauer)
- US 3rd Army (Patton)
  - US 14 Armored Division (Smith)
  - US VIII Corps (Middleton)
    - US 4 Infantry Division (Blakely)
    - US 87 Infantry Division (Culin)
    - US 90 Infantry Division (Van Fleet)
    - US 6 Armored Division (Grow)
    - US 11 Armored Division (Kilburn)
  - US XII Corps (Eddy)
    - US 5 Infantry Division (Irwin)
    - US 76 Infantry Division (Schmidt)
    - US 80 Infantry Division (McBride)
    - US 89 Infantry Division (Finley)
    - US 4 Armored Division (Gaffoy)
  - US XX Corps (Walker)
    - US 26 Infantry Division (Paul)
    - US 65 Infantry Division (Reinhart)
    - US 94 Infantry Division (Malony)
    - US 10 Armored Division (Morris)

US 6th Army Group (Devers)
- US 7th Army (Patch)
  - US 12 Armored Division (Allen)
  - US VI Corps (Brooks)
    - US 36 Infantry Division (Dahlquist)
    - US 42 Infantry Division (Collins)
    - US 44 Infantry Division (Dean)
    - US 103 Infantry Division (McAulife)
    - Algerian 3 Infantry Division (Gillaume)
  - US XV Corps (Haislip)
    - US 3 Infantry Division (O'Daniel)
    - US 45 Infantry Division (Frederick)
    - US 63 Infantry Division (Hibbs)
    - US 100 Infantry Division (Burress)
- French 1st Army (de Tassigny)
  - French 27 Alpine Division (Molle)
  - French 1 Infantry Division (Garbay)
  - French 2 Armored Division (Leclerc)
  - French I Corps (Béthouart)
    - French 4 Mountain Division (De Hesdin)
    - French 9 Colonial Infantry Division (Valluy)
    - French 14 Infantry Division (Salan)
    - French 1 Armoured Division (Sudre)
  - French II Corps (De Montsabert)
    - Moroccan 2 Infantry Division (Carpentier)
    - French 5 Armored Division (De Vernejoul)

British 21st Army Group (Montgomery)
- British 2nd Army (Dempsey)
  - British 79 Armoured Division (Hobart)
  - British I Corps (Crocker)
    - British 49 Infantry Division (MacMillan)
    - Polish 1 Armoured Division (Maczek)
  - British VIII Corps (Barker)
    - British 3 Infantry Division (Whistler)
    - British 11 Armoured Division (Roberts)
  - British XII Corps (Ritchie)
    - British 52 (Lowland) Division (Hakewill Smith)
    - British 7th Armoured Division (Lyne)

- Canadian 1st Army (Crerar)
  - British XXX Corps (Horrocks)
    - British 15 (Scottish) Division (Barber)
    - British 43 (Wessex) Division (Thomas)
    - British 51 (Highland) Division (Rennie)
    - British 53 (Welsh) Division (Ross)
    - British Guards Armoured Division (Adair)
    - Canadian 2 Infantry Division (Matthews)
    - Canadian 3 Infantry Division (Spry)
  - Canadian II Corps (Simonds)
    - Canadian 4 Armored Division (Vokes)
- US 9th Army (Simpson)
  - US 75 Infantry Division (Porter)
  - US 95 Infantry Division (Twadle)
  - US XVI Corps (Anderson)
    - US 35 Infantry Division (Baade)
    - US 79 Infantry Division (Wyche)
    - US 8 Armored Division (Devine)
  - US XIII Corps (Gillem)
    - US 84 Infantry Division (Bolling)
    - US 102 Infantry Division (Keating)
    - US 5 Armored Division (Oliver)
  - US XIX Corps (McLain)
    - US 29 Infantry Division (Gerhardt)
    - US 30 Infantry Division (Hobbs)
    - US 83 Infantry Division (Macon)
    - US 2 Armored Division (White)

Air support
- British RAF
  - 2nd Tactical Air Force
- French
  - 1st Air Corps
- American
  - IX, XII, XIX, XXIX Tactical Air Command
  - IX US Bomber Command
  - US Eighth Air Force

NOTE: These Allied groupings were as existed for the opening of the 'Veritable' 'Grenade' operations early in February 1945. During this period, many units were being earmarked and shifted to new sectors at short notice as the situation demanded.

SELECTED BIBLIOGRAPHY

Allen, Peter *One More River,* JM Dent, 1980

Barclay, Brig CN *The History of the 53rd (Welsh) Division in the Second World War,* William Clowes, 1956

Blake, George *Mountain and Flood,* Jackson & Son & Company, 1950

Draper, Lt Theodore *The 84th Infantry Division in the Battle Of Germany,* Viking Press, New York, 1946

Elstob, Peter *The Battle Of The Reichswald,* Macdonald, 1970

Essame, MajGen H The 43rd *Wessex Division at War 1939–1945,* William Clowes, 1952

Essame, MajGen H *The Battle For Germany,* Batsford, 1969

Horrocks, LtGen Sir Brian *Corps Commander,* Sidgwick & Jackson, 1977

MacDonald, Charles B *The Last Offensive,* Washington, DC, 1951

MacDonald, Charles B *The Siegfried Line Campaign,* Washington DC, 1963

Martin, LtGen HG *The History of the Fifteenth Scottish Division 1939–1945,* William Blackwood, 1948

Mitcham, Samuel W *Hitler's Legions,* Leo Cooper, 1985

Salmond, JB *The History of the 51st Highland Division 1939–1945,* William Blackwood, 1953

Weigley, Russell F *Eisenhower's Lieutenants,* Sidgwick & Jackson, 1981

Whitaker, WD & S *Rhineland: The Battle To End The War,* Leo Cooper, 1989

Whiting, Charles *Siegfried,* Leo Cooper, 1983

Williams, Jeffery *The Long Left Flank,* Leo Cooper, 1988

A machine-gun crew of the US 9th Army looks out across the River Rhine from a captured barn. The Browning 0.5 inch (12.7mm) M2 (HB) heavy machine gun had been in American service since 1921 and became one of the best anti-personnel weapons ever used. It was also capable of firing armour-piercing rounds. In this picture, the crew were using the gun's effective range of over 2,000 yards (1,820m) to provide interdictory fire against enemy movements across the river. (National Archives, Washington)

WARGAMING THE CAMPAIGN

Most wargamers who recreate the battles of the Western Front on the tabletop tend to concentrate on the larger, more publicised campaigns, such as the battle for Normandy, Operation Market Garden and the Battle of the Bulge. In the past few years a new series of Divisional histories, books covering more obscure battles (such as the Overloon salient, the campaign for the Schelde or the battle for Aachen) and research information via the Internet have helped make minor battles more accessible to wargamers. The battle for the Rhineland is a fascinating source of inspiration for miniature gamers, and this book provides information on dozens of actions which would translate well onto the tabletop.

Gaming with Miniature Figurines

For several years, the most popular set of wargame rules for Divisional or Brigade-sized games was *Command Decision*, which replaced the earlier Wargames Research Group rules as the standard within the hobby. In the last few years *Command Decision* had evolved through three editions, each becoming more elaborate (and complex). At the same time, their position was challenged by *Spearhead*, a set which mirrored the basic simplicity of the *Command Decision* playing system, but which introduced new approaches to wargaming in the period. Both sets are sound, playable rules systems, and although both can be slowed down by the use of additional or special rules, experienced gamers can play a fast-moving and enjoyable game with them. While primarily designed for 1:300 or 1:285 scale figures, they are both equally suitable for 10mm or 15mm scales, although less than ideal for anything larger.

An ideal multi-player game on this scale would be the struggle to capture Goch. Although the attack on 19 February involved three British divisions, only three brigades spearheaded the attack. While the defenders benefited from strong defences and interior lines of communication, the overwhelming artillery firepower of the British proved decisive. A game where each Allied player has set objectives, and an overall commander allocates corps level resources would recreate the command structure of the battle, although for the German player his options are more limited, and his objective would be survival, or even the successful extrication of his forces while causing high casualties to the attacker. At this stage of the war British manpower reserves were drained, and heavy losses were unacceptable, and should be reflected in the victory conditions.

Other suitable games on this scale could be the attack by the 43rd (Wessex) Division towards the Goch–Calcar road, the Roer crossings by Simpson's 9th Army or the reduction of the Xanten pocket. Each has its own interesting features; a classical divisional attack where the British

American dead from the first waves of the 84th Division's assault crossing of the River Roer at Linnich. The paddle-powered storm boat was swept by German machine-gun fire as the infantry tried to reach the far side of the swiftly flowing river. Despite several of the boats being caught by German fire, casualties were relatively light for such a complex operation.
(National Archives, Washington)

commander showed unusual flair in the juggling of his forces, a river crossing under enemy fire and the grinding reduction of an enemy bridgehead, while the defender tries to extricate whatever troops he can. The beauty of this level of gaming is that it allows for logistical considerations to enter into the game. The account of the drive on Cleve where two divisions shared the same muddy road is an example of the importance of logistics, and can be represented by special rules governing the arrival (or non-arrival) of reinforcements and ammunition.

While these larger Divisional actions are best suited for large games involving several players, this level of wargame is perfect for two opponents. As most of the engagements fought during this campaign were fought on the brigade level, this provides the best scope for wargamers. While there are several commercial rules sets available, one of the most popular is *Rapid Fire*, a simple and elegant set of rules which are reminiscent of the Charles Grant *Battle* rules of the 1970s. Designed for 15mm and 20mm figures, games using *Rapid Fire* are consistently fun, fast moving and a pleasure to play. While they lack the detailed command and control rules of the larger sets, a recent *Operation Market Garden* supplement included suggestions for a command structure.

An unusual brigade-level action would be the initial attacks in the Reichswald by the 51st (Highland) Division and 53rd (Welsh) Division; assaults made in atrocious conditions, where contact between the units of the attacking force was almost impossible. Suitable limitations will need to be imposed on the units, virtually fighting 'blind' through the dense Reichswald forest. Other ideal brigade scenarios would be the

ABOVE **A modern view of the edge of the Reichswald at the point where the 53rd (Welsh) Division entered the woods. The road turns sharply to the left in the distance, just in front of the trees, where it is joined by one of the major rides through the forest. This track served as the main axis for the 53rd Division's advance and was code-named 'Maine'. The rising ground of the Brandenberg feature can be made out above the top of the trees. (Norbert Rosin)**

RIGHT **Dragon's teeth marking an anti-tank section of the Siegfried Line stretch across a modern farm to the north of Aachen. Most of Hitler's Westwall defences have disappeared but it is still possible to come across some remnants of the fortifications in the Rhineland area. (Author)**

night battle in the streets of Cleve by a brigade of the 43rd (Wessex) Division, the later drive through the Reichswald, and any of the Roer river crossings by Simpson's 9th Army. The conditions facing the British need to be recreated; mud too thick to allow armour support, continual rain (and consequently poor visibility) and a lack of logistical support. It is precisely these challenges which makes the Rhineland operation so fascinating to refight.

For years there were no commercial rules available which covered this level of gaming. This has now changed, and in the last couple of years *Crossfire* and *Battleground* have both filled the void. Other less commercially popular sets are also available. Of the two, *Crossfire* has the more elegant games system, using a unique method of adjudicating movement and

The derelict brick viaduct leading to the rail bridge across the River Rhine at Wesel still stands after 54 years of redundancy. The bridge was blown, along with the road bridge half a mile upstream, just before Montgomery's 21st Army Group reached the river. (Norbert Rosin)

combat. It produces a tense, enjoyable game, and the system lends itself perfectly to certain aspects of the Rhineland campaign. *Battleground* places a greater emphasis on hardware (tanks, weapons etc.) and although slower, it produces a highly realistic game.

The amphibious operations conducted by the 3rd Canadian Division to the north of the main Operation Veritable battleground provide a highly unusual battalion-level game. German-held villages became island strongpoints, and these were assaulted by battalion-sized Canadian units riding in amphibious carriers. Players may have to adapt special rules to suit the circumstances, reflecting the shock-effect of these amphibious assaults, and the concentrated barrages which preceded them. The assault of the Wiltshire battalions near Tippenburg, or the following day's action by the Somersets are both prime examples of British battalion-level attacks; rigid start-lines, limited objectives and supporting armour and artillery fire. By contrast, the river crossings by units of the American 84th Division and the subsequent exploitation of their bridgehead was a far more impromptu affair, particularly the assault on Korrenzig village by the I/334th Battalion. The terrain which formed the battleground for the latter action makes a refight using rules such as *Crossfire* particularly rewarding.

Skirmish Games

There are too many sets of skirmish-level rules to name, but most Second World War sets place an emphasis on equipment and squad-level tactics. Although excellent for recreating the constant patrolling during any phase of the war, skirmish-level games are also suitable for refighting several of the actions of the Rhineland campaign. For example, the patrol by Lt Roy Rogers across the Roer River to silence German machine guns is a fascinating subject for a skirmish game, as is the race to secure the Roer Dams before they could be destroyed. Similarly, the rapid advance made by Patton's 3rd Army through the Saarland during

March 1945 left numerous groups of German soldiers isolated behind American lines. While many simply surrendered, others tried to rejoin their units, providing a suitably compelling background for a skirmish game. The whole Rhineland campaign contains engagements worthy of refighting at almost every level, from divisional down to the actions of individual squads. The secret is to adapt whatever rules you use to reflect the particular circumstances of the Rhineland battles: mud, rain and a dogged defence.

The Reichswald, unchanged after 54 years. The picture shows one of the major cross tracks in the 51st (Highland) Division's sector. (Author)

Board and Computer Games

Although no board wargames deal directly with the campaign, several portray the larger campaign in north-west Europe. The flavour of the latter stages of the war is admirably caught in the old SPI game *Battle for Germany*, where the player takes either the Russian or the Allied army, plus the German defenders facing the troops of his opponent. In recent years board wargames have been partly eclipsed by computer wargames, and several provide an excellent vehicle for refighting the campaign. Of these the most accurate is *The Operational Art of War, Volume 1*, a clumsy title for a superb wargame. Only one of the initial scenarios included with the game relates to this phase of fighting in north-west Europe, but a scenario design package is also included in the game. Players can also download extra scenarios from several free web sites, and these include ones featuring the Rhineland battles. Although the game is flexible, most scenarios concentrate on the army group level, and the players move battalion-sized units. Another popular computer game is *West Front*, fought at a brigade level, and each unit represents a platoon. Once again, the initial range of scenarios are augmented by additional games which can be downloaded. These include the battle for the Reichswald and the capture of Düren by the US VII Corps. On an even smaller scale, *Steel Panthers* provides a playable game where each infantry squad and individual tank is represented. Like the previous games, downloaded scenarios from the Internet provide a greater range than the designers included with the initial game, and a design package allows gamers to create their own scenarios.

BELOW **Infantry from the Canadian 3rd Division pass through a flooded village whilst securing the extreme left side of the Canadian 1st Army's sector. The rising water from the blown dykes on the Rhine and Maas rivers had inundated miles of open countryside, leaving isolated villages protruding from the water. These groups of houses had often been reinforced by German defenders to form strong points from which they threatened the flanks of Operation 'Veritable'.** (Imperial War Museum)

INDEX

COMPANION SERIES FROM OSPREY

MEN-AT-ARMS

An unrivalled source of information on the organisation, uniforms and equipment of the world's fighting men, past and present. The series covers hundreds of subjects spanning 5,000 years of history. Each 48-page book includes concise texts packed with specific information, some 40 photos, maps and diagrams, and eight colour plates of uniformed figures.

ELITE

Detailed information on the uniforms and insignia of the world's most famous military forces. Each 64-page book contains some 50 photographs and diagrams, and 12 pages of full-colour artwork.

NEW VANGUARD

Comprehensive histories of the design, development and operational use of the world's armoured vehicles and artillery. Each 48-page book contains eight pages of full-colour artwork including a detailed cutaway.

WARRIOR

Definitive analysis of the armour, weapons, tactics and motivation of the fighting men of history. Each 64-page book contains cutaways and exploded artwork of the warrior's weapons and armour.

ORDER OF BATTLE

The most detailed information ever published on the units which fought history's great battles. Each 96-page book contains comprehensive organisation diagrams supported by ultra-detailed colour maps. Each title also includes a large fold-out base map.

AIRCRAFT OF THE ACES

Focuses exclusively on the elite pilots of major air campaigns, and includes unique interviews with surviving aces sourced specifically for each volume. Each 96-page volume contains up to 40 specially commissioned artworks, unit listings, new scale plans and the best archival photography available.

COMBAT AIRCRAFT

Technical information from the world's leading aviation writers on the aircraft types flown. Each 96-page volume contains up to 40 specially commissioned artworks, unit listings, new scale plans and the best archival photography available.